The Other Side of Suffering

LARGE PRINT EDITION

The Other Side of Suffering

The Father of JonBenét Ramsey Tells the Story of His Journey from Grief to Grace

John Ramsey

with Marie Chapian

New York Boston Nashville

LARGE PRINT EDITION

The author is represented by Alive Communications, Inc., 7680 Goddard Street, Suite 200, Colorado Springs, CO 80920, www.alivecommunications.com.

Unless otherwise indicated, Scriptures are taken from the New King James Version®. Copyright © 1982 by Thomas Nelson, Inc. Used by permission. All rights reserved.

Scriptures noted NIV are taken from the HOLY BIBLE, NEW INTERNATIONAL VERSION®. Copyright © 1973, 1978, 1984 by International Bible Society. Used by permission of Zondervan. All rights reserved.

Scriptures noted KJV are taken from the King James Version of the Bible.

Copyright © 2012 by John Ramsey

All rights reserved. In accordance with the U.S. Copyright Act of 1976, the scanning, uploading, and electronic sharing of any part of this book without the permission of the publisher is unlawful piracy and theft of the author's intellectual property. If you would like to use material from the book (other than for review purposes), prior written permission must be obtained by contacting the publisher at permissions@hbgusa.com. Thank you for your support of the author's rights.

FaithWords
Hachette Book Group
237 Park Avenue
New York, NY 10017

www.faithwords.com

Printed in the United States of America

First Edition: March 2012

10 9 8 7 6 5 4 3 2 1

FaithWords is a division of Hachette Book Group, Inc.
The FaithWords name and logo are trademarks of Hachette Book Group, Inc.

The publisher is not responsible for websites (or their content) that are not owned by the publisher.

Library of Congress Cataloging-in-Publication Data

Ramsey, John.
 The other side of suffering : the father of JonBenét Ramsey tells the story of his journey from grief to grace / John Ramsey, with Marie Chapian. — 1st ed.
   p. cm.
 ISBN 978-0-89296-385-0 (hc) / 978-1-4555-4586-5 (lp)
 1. Ramsey, John. 2. Ramsey, JonBenét, d. p. 3. Murder—Colorado—Boulder—Case studies. 4. Fathers of murder victims—United States—Biography. 5. Spirituality. I. Chapian, Marie. II. Title.
HV6534.B73R354 2012
362.88—dc23
[B]   2011023225

*Many men owe the grandeur of their lives
to their tremendous suffering.*
—Charles Spurgeon

Contents

    Preface   ix
1. *Struck by Evil*   1
2. *Messages from Heaven*   17
3. *Why Suffering?*   27
4. *Life in Chaos*   33
5. *Angels*   40
6. *Spiritual Roadblocks*   55
7. *Faith Under Fire*   62
8. *God and Healing*   70
9. *Love, Divorce, and Grace*   79
10. *Regrets*   88
11. *Trusting God*   97
12. *All Things for Good?*   108
13. *God's Promises*   113
14. *God Working Through People*   123
15. *The Power of Choice*   137
16. *Resilience of the Spirit*   145
17. *Saying Good-bye*   154

18. The Greatest of Christian Promises   163
19. DNA Points JonBenét's Case in a New Direction   168
20. Forgiveness: A Gift to Ourselves   172
21. Are the Best Days Ahead?   177
22. The Problem of Pride   182
23. Getting Close to God   187
24. Learning Discipleship   193
25. Dream of Flying   199
26. Changing Perspectives   204
27. Are Demons Real?   211
28. A Man's Legacy   215
29. Stopping the Fall   220
30. Engaging in Life Again   227
31. Becoming a Whole Person   232
32. Touches from God   235
33. Can I Be Happy Again?   237
34. A New Beginning   240
    Appendix   243

Preface

My life has been often grueling and complex over the past fifteen years. I'm a simple businessman who lost children, wife, much of my life savings, and my good reputation. In 1996, JonBenét, my precious six-year-old little girl, was violently murdered in our home on Christmas night as we slept in our beds. I was placed under an "umbrella of suspicion" as being her killer. My gentle, loving wife, battling ovarian cancer, was publicly placed under the same umbrella.

   The world media was quick to sensationalize our tragedy and led a tabloid-fueled frenzy that sought our conviction for the murder of our child. What most people do not know is my world had nearly collapsed four years earlier when my oldest daughter, Beth, was killed in a car accident.

For some time I've felt compelled to share my untold faith journey to help and encourage fellow strugglers. I've learned that almost no one escapes scars from loss, unfairness, abuse, or heartbreak. I want to share with you how I recovered and reestablished a direction for my life, and hope for the future. Most important, I want to tell you how my faith in God was tremendously strengthened. It's my prayer that my personal story might help and encourage you on your life journey.

This is the story you have never heard.

Delhi, India—December 31, 2009

It's late evening. I've missed my connection to Bangalore, and the next flight won't leave until nine thirty in the morning. It will be a lonely New Year's Eve for sure. I can feel myself having what my wife, Patsy, and I used to call a pity party, feeling sorry for ourselves. I walk outside the airport into the Delhi night air, damp with fog generated by the cool evening air and the closeness to the Himalayas. It smells of a peculiar mixture of aging fruit and diesel exhaust—not a bad odor, just an aroma unique to India, I'd soon learn. I begin walking in the direction the ticket agent said: "You'll find a hotel just outside, turn to the left, down a few blocks..." I need the exercise, and with these marginal directions, a taxi is probably out of the question, so I start walking, as the man said, just outside, turn to the left...

The noise and clamor of travelers of every race and nationality hustle for taxis and rickshaws; uniformed police blow whistles and wave their arms; crowds of men, women, and children stand in queues and restless clumps waiting for buses.

I collide with an old Indian man struggling with a large suitcase wrapped in twine. He moves slowly, his back bent over in an obvious state of scoliosis, his body a cascade of bones beneath his neatly wrapped tunic. He's barefoot, his right foot slightly twisted and crippled, and he walks one hesitant step at a time. The turban on his head is brown with dust, his beard a tangled series of knots. He is startled by our abrupt meeting and has the look of someone almost overwhelmed by life. He could be someone's grandfather. He stumbles and the old suitcase falls to the ground. I feel like I should do something, so I reach down to help right the suitcase. "Sorry, let me give you a hand." He smiles at me with a subservient, toothless smile exaggerated by his emaciated features.

He doesn't respond to my offer for help, but continues smiling, his brown skin creased, burnt like crushed cardboard. He peers up at me, giving me a look as though we have connected in a strange way. The smile seems personal, as though we share a private secret.

"Please, let me help you with that—"

I reach for his suitcase, but he hangs on tight. It's obvious he doesn't speak English. He clings to the suitcase with both arms, shielding it from me. His smell is almost overpowering, acrid, pungent, as though he hasn't taken a bath in months. I look into his eyes and realize the left one is blind, a milky veil covering the pupil in spongy blankness. The other eye gleams like black onyx, and I feel it penetrate into my own. He continues to stare at me, smiling, while protecting his suitcase.

I feel somehow connected to this man. Is he a beggar? A vendor? A traveler? Who is he? I'm aware that the cities in India are full of beggars. Men, women, and children with desperate lives. He hobbles to the edge of the walkway and unties the frayed twine around the battered suitcase. Inside is a small rug and what appear to be a few dozen clay amulets. He rolls the rug out on the worn dirt and sits on it, his legs crossed with the crippled foot twisted upward. He spreads out the amulets before him, closes the suitcase, the whole time watching me with his one good eye and smiling that smile.

How does he do it? I wonder. How does he manage to go on with life when he's old, crippled, half blind, and destitute?

People have asked me, "John, how have you survived all your suffering?"

Here is a man that makes my struggles look easy. What motivates him to continue living?

His mouth is dry and peeling; his smile reveals blackened gums. I'm filled with feelings I can't identify, and on the crowded, noisy street by the Delhi airport, I ask him, "How do you go on?"

He nods, the grin spreads. We can't communicate with words. He probably speaks Hindi, the official language of India.

For the last few years, I've lived through overwhelming loss and I've come to India battered and bruised by the world, but with a growing faith in God. I've learned a lot about my faith since its fragile underpinnings were rocked to the core eighteen years ago.

I'm seeking His direction for my life. I wonder what faith, if any, this man has. He must have some sort of faith. Probably Hindu, since 85 percent of India is Hindu. The remainder is split between Christian, Muslim, and Buddhist. Hindus have thousands of gods they worship. The caste system, which was outlawed by the government years ago, is still very alive in practice. This man no doubt is a Dalit, or untouchable, the lowest caste.

I've just spent two months of classroom study at a discipleship training school in Hawaii called Youth With A Mission, or YWAM. This part of our practical training is to work among the poorest of the poor in India, supporting local Indian pastors who work tirelessly to minister to these people.

I kneel down as the man holds out an amulet to me, places it in my hand. Is it a gift? Of course not. I tell him, "Thanks but I'm traveling with only a duffel bag and backpack and I don't have room for one more thing." Besides, I've been downsizing my life over the past ten years, and I don't want to start accumulating things again. The man clicks his tongue. He has no idea what I'm saying. He pats my hand and strokes my arm with two weathered fingers.

I look at this man and realize I'm someone like him, really, in a way, aren't I? A struggler in life? Granted, I'm not blind or crippled, but we're both out here making our way in a difficult world.

I'm still holding the amulet. I pull out a five-dollar bill from my pocket and give it to him. I haven't had time to get rupees, and five dollars could be a small fortune to him.

"God bless you," I tell him, and I place the amulet back on his rug.

He face erupts in another grin and he places his hands together and gives me a rapid series of bows.

I have an urge to stay and talk to him, this man who can't understand me. His one glittering eye tells me he might be listening.

Feeling awkward, I finally say good-bye, leave him there, and continue walking. When at last I come upon the hotel, I'm sweating and my sinuses feel stuffed with wool. The hotel clerk hands me a key to a room and I fall onto a thin, worn-out mattress in a windowless room protected by a door with an antique lock.

The question still stirs in my head. How does he have the will to get up in the morning, that old man? What is there to live for when you're old, half blind, and crippled with only a rug and some clay souvenirs to sell?

I'll be here in India for two months on this mission trip. I pray to be useful. I traveled eight thousand miles to India to be a blessing. I would have gladly sat down on the ground with that old man and talked to him about life and faith. More important, I wish I could know his story. Perhaps I could learn from him, this man who once was an innocent child and now carries the scars of life.

Lord, am I ready for this?

The Other Side of Suffering

CHAPTER 1

Struck by Evil

Let the little children come to Me.
—Matthew 19:14

I'll start with Christmas.
Because I must.

The long anticipated day after weeks of shopping, decorating, preparing, this exciting festive day finally arrived. Our children were first to rise in the early hours of the morning to rush up the stairs to our third-floor bedroom in our home in Boulder, Colorado, and wake us up with squeals of excitement. JonBenét, our six-year-old daughter, jumped on my chest. "Daddy, wake up, wake up! It's Christmas!" It was 1996.

Patsy smiled at me as Burke, our nine-year-old son, and JonBenét jumped on the end of the bed. "Meeerrrrry Christmas!" I reached for them, and the four of us rolled about on the bed hugging, laughing, tickling, and excited about the day at hand.

"Santa's been here, I know it!" JonBenét exclaimed. "Come on, you guys. Let's go see!" and with a tug and a yank, we were out of bed to go check out what Santa had brought this year.

There's something so wonderful about children who've just awakened, tousled and warm in their pajamas, smelling of sleep. I felt a sense of deep contentment watching them bound down the stairs to the living room, where they'd discover their presents under the enormous Fraser fir Christmas tree. "Come on, Daddy!"

It was my job to plug in the Christmas tree lights, turn on the Christmas music, and get the camera set up. I decided not to be the photographer this year because I wanted to be part of the festivities, not just an observer. Of all times not to video. I've regretted that.

Our rule was no presents until the tree lights were lit and the music was playing. "Hurry up, Daddy!"

People always say Christmas is for children, and Patsy and I tried to make it just that. We celebrated the birth of Jesus, sang carols, gave parties and dinners, and bought gifts, and the children performed in their school programs. This year they were both in the Annual Children's Christmas Parade, which wove around downtown Boulder.

Christmas was going to be extra special this year because the morning after, on the twenty-sixth, we planned to fly to our vacation home in Michigan to celebrate the holidays with my son and daughter from my first marriage, John Andrew and Melinda. They were flying in from Atlanta. We would then ring in the new year and Patsy's birthday on December twenty-ninth on the Disney Big Red Boat. It would be our first cruise ever, and it was chosen to be something special for the kids. I wasn't sure if hanging around with Mickey Mouse was going to be fun for me, but I knew it would be wonderful to see my children having a great time.

On Christmas Eve, we'd hauled all the gifts up from the basement, where Patsy had wrapped and hidden them. We bought a new bicycle for JonBenét, which we kept out of sight at our neighbor's, a Nintendo 64 video game for Burke, and heaped around the tree were the many toys and gifts from our families. It had been a full day with last-minute preparations—Christmas Eve service at church, then out to dinner at Pasta Jay's, and our annual drive around town to admire the lights, with the crowning stop at the top of Flagstaff Mountain to the lighted star that shines down on the city.

Patsy bought a My Twinn doll from a doll maker who specialized in creating dolls from photographs to look like the child who would own it. She had been thrilled to find this doll maker, and even bought a couple of matching outfits so JonBenét and the doll could dress alike. JonBenét opened the box Christmas morning, took one look, and wrinkled her nose. "Thanks, Mommy," she said politely, but we could tell she was more interested in other toys.

Patsy shrugged, then examined the doll in the box and gave a shudder. Leaning toward me, she whispered, "John, this doll lying in the box like this with her blond hair spread out and eyes closed—my gosh, it looks like a child in a casket! It kind of gives me the creeps."

I gave the box only a quick glance, because I was preoccupied with watching Burke unwrap the dark green Pontiac GTO remote-control car I had chosen for him. Later Patsy remembered the life-sized doll and agonized that perhaps it had been a warning. If it was a warning, it went right over our heads. We were too busy being happy.

JonBenét had chosen a surprise for me and insisted I open it first. When she had taken a trip to New York City earlier in the year with her mother, they visited FAO Schwarz, where she spotted a gumball machine that popped out jellybeans. "Daddy has to have that!" she exclaimed to her mother. "Daddy loves jelly beans!" She and Patsy had kept it a secret until now, and I was really touched. "Honey, it's the best present ever. Thank you!"

Hugs and more hugs. Presents and more presents. Oohs and ahhs and more oohs and ahhs. Thank-yous and wows. A gold chain with a gold cross for JonBenét, which she insisted on wearing immediately. A gold bracelet with her name and 12-25-96 inscribed on it. Gene Autry in the background singing "Rudolph the Red-Nosed Reindeer." Then our traditional Christmas breakfast. I made the pancakes; the kids decorated them with raisins, fruit, chocolate chips, and colored sprinkles; and Mom cooked the bacon and the corned beef hash. *"...had a very shiny noooose..."*

JonBenét was the chef's helper in every aspect, perched on a kitchen stool, stirring pancake batter, scooping it onto the griddle. As usual, the kids barely touched their food because they were far more interested in playing with their new toys scattered around the living room than wasting too much time eating.

Patsy and I sipped our coffee in the living room and watched them happily play with their abundance of new toys. I gave Patsy a kiss and thanked her for making this another extraordinary and beautiful Christmas. "Oh, sweetie," she said, snuggling against me in her cozy terry cloth robe, "you're the one who makes it all possible, you know."

Everything is for my family, I thought to myself. For this. This moment. This contentment. There is no treasure on earth that could weigh in with more value or worth than this, living in a home filled with love. If I could arrest time, it would be this moment. My children, my wife, and I on an early Christmas morning, the smells of pine and cinnamon and fried corned beef hash floating in the air, hundreds of sparkling lights on the Christmas tree, and jubilant children; candles, happy music, *"Then how the reindeer loved him as they shouted out with glee..."* The world at peace.

A perfect Christmas.

Our family wasn't perfect by any means. Maybe we overdid Christmas. Maybe all the gifts were too much. JonBenét was the typical little sister to her big brother, Burke. Often an annoyance as he built his Lego projects. But this morning everything was as perfect as we could make it.

JonBenét couldn't wait to try out her new bicycle. "Daddy, can I ride now? Now?" We threw on our jackets and off we went for her first expedition on a bicycle pedaling by herself around the block. I held on to the handle bar and seat as she pedaled, and you would have thought she was captain of the *Enterprise.* "Look at me, Daddy! Look at me!"

"You're doing great, Johnnie Bee!"

She could have pedaled around the block all day. "Let's go again, Daddy!"

"No, honey, not now. Maybe later."

"Please, Daddy? Pretty please?"

"No, we don't have time."

So much to do before we were to take off the next morning for Michigan. Packing winter clothes for cold weather, as well as summer clothes for the Disney cruise. Gifts left to wrap for Melinda and John Andrew, more gifts to bring for neighbors, friends of the kids, as well as Melinda's fiancé, Stewart, who would be spending his first Christmas with our family. Melinda had just finished nursing school and started her career as a neonatal intensive care nurse.

And we'd promised to attend dinner at our friends' house a few blocks away. I lose my breath as I say these words. If this were a movie, the sound track would now become dissonant, ominous, deathly—foreshadowing disaster. We left our house. Did we leave a light on? I can't remember.

We were gone a few hours. Just a few hours.

Enough time for someone to crawl through a broken basement window, select a hiding place, write a ransom note, and wait.

We walked out our door, merrily piled into the family car with our gifts and Christmas cookies, and—left our house.

We left our home.

No burglar alarm set, every window and door unchecked.

We drive to the home of our friends. We eat special Christmas treats, talk to relatives from California, enjoy our friends; the kids play and make Christmas crafts, and we leave around eight thirty in the evening; happy but tired now, having gotten up at the crack of dawn. We drop off gifts to more friends on the way home and drive down the decorated streets of Boulder, a town where most everyone owns a bicycle, a town surrounded by more than thirty-six thousand acres of recreational open space, conservation easements, and nature preserves. A seemingly idyllic town tucked neatly below the iconic rock formations of the Flatiron Mountains. A city of old hippies, successful businesspeople, philanthropists, trust fund babies, families, children, the University of Colorado, and world-class hiking trails, parks, and rock climbing. We drive along Baseline at the edge of the university campus to 15th Street, Patsy exclaiming how pretty the lights are. "Oh, John, I love Christmas!" Such a seemingly perfect city, where unknown to us, more than forty registered sex offenders live within five blocks of our house.

The kids are sleepy in the backseat. Patsy and I are tired, glad to get home early knowing we have to rise early in the morning to be at the Jefferson County airport for takeoff at 7 a.m.

JonBenét is sound asleep when I pull the car into the darkened alley behind our house and into the garage. The driveway is clean and dry. I am relieved as it bodes well for a fair-weather takeoff in the morning. It's around 9 p.m.

I bundle JonBenét in my arms and carry her inside and upstairs to her room on the second floor. She is so light in my arms, her sturdy little legs in her boots bouncing over my arm. I lay her down on her bed and think to myself that one of these days she'll be too big to carry—one of these days she'll be all grown up, kids grow up so fast. I kiss her on the forehead, smooth her hair, and tiptoe out of the room. Patsy will come up in a few minutes and get her into her pajamas.

Burke plays downstairs in the living room by the Christmas tree. He's trying to assemble a mechanical robot made of the Legos he got for Christmas, so I sit down on the floor to help him put it together, but it's way too complicated for tonight.

"Son, it's time for bed."

"Do I have to go to bed?"

"Yes, buddy. Five-thirty will come mighty quick. Come on, I'll tuck you in."

Burke and I climb upstairs to his room, which is on the other side of the playroom from JonBenét's room. I help get him ready for bed, tuck him under the covers, and give him a kiss on the forehead. "You're a good son, Burke. I love you."

"I love you, too, Dad."

I feel good. My children are safe in their beds, the activities of the day are over, Patsy and I are exhausted, but once again it has been a Christmas to remember. I crawl into bed, adjust my favorite pillow, and promptly fall asleep.

A sound sleep I will forever regret.

It's still dark when I roll out of bed the following morning and head for the shower. The morning winter air coming from our slightly cracked open bedroom window is crisp, clean. Outside the stars show through broken clouds, and grass, brittle and sullen, peeks through open patches in the snow; the city lies sleeping in the profile of the mountains and twinkling Christmas lights left on all night. Patsy had decorated every room in our house for Christmas, and outside had lined the walk with candy canes, and hung wreaths in the windows and on the six exterior doors on the first floor. *Spectacular* is a word you could use when describing any project Patsy set her hand to. Our house with its wreaths and centerpieces and candles and trinkets and trees and baubles and statues and crèches and lighted angels and Santas and reindeer and gingerbread sculptures was color coordinated, perfectly arranged and done with her elegant, and sometimes flamboyant, taste. People are impressed, but that's not Patsy's objective, to impress people. Her lively extroverted personality just happens to come through everything she does. I'm used to it. I know she can make an art out of just about anything.

Some people, however, are not always all that impressed with Patsy's creative talents. In 1995, two thousand people went through our Christmas house, which Patsy had decorated to support a fund-raiser for the Boulder Historical Society. I stood outside wondering what to do with myself, when a woman emerged from our front door with a frown on her face.

"Well, how did you like it?" someone nearby asked her.

"It's disgusting!" she exclaimed. Then to me, she said, "Have you ever seen such *excess*? It's a disgrace!" and off she huffed.

"Excess?" Patsy marveled. "Maybe, but if people are going to pay money to see Christmas decorations, I'm going to give them their money's worth!" And she did. For politically correct Boulder, I guess we overdid it.

But now it's the morning after Christmas. I hear Patsy in her bathroom getting dressed. Then she's down the stairs to put on the coffee, gather our things. We'll wait to wake the kids until the last minute, taking them in the car in their PJs like we've done before so they can sleep on the plane.

A shriek. More like a howl. "John! *Johhhn!*"

I drop my razor, rush to the head of the stairs. "What is it?"

"JonBenét! JonBenét's gone!"

"John, I found a note on the stairs! It's a ransom note!" She screams, frantic. "John! There's a note!"

She rushes to JonBenét's room and through the playroom to Burke's room and I follow. Burke is sleeping peacefully in his bed, but JonBenét is gone.

"Someone has taken JonBenét!" Patsy shrieks. I hurl myself down the spiral stairs to the back hallway, scoop up the three-page ransom note on the steps, and spread the sheets on the floor. I try and take in all three pages at once. I drop to my knees and read:

Mr. Ramsey,
Listen carefully! We are a group of individuals that represent a small foreign faction. We

respect your business but not the country that it serves. At this time we have your daughter in our possession. She is safe and unharmed and if you want her to see 1997, you must follow our instructions to the letter.

You will withdraw $118,000.00 from your account. $100,000 will be in $100 bills and the remaining $18,000 in $20 bills. Make sure that you bring an adequate size attaché to the bank. When you get home you will put the money in a brown paper bag. I will call you between 8 and 10 am tomorrow to instruct you on delivery. The delivery will be exhausting so I advise you to be rested. If we monitor you getting the money early, we might call you early to arrange an earlier delivery of the money and hence an earlier pick-up of your daughter.

Any deviation of my instructions will result in the immediate execution of your daughter. You will also be denied her remains for proper burial. The two gentlemen watching over your daughter do not particularly like you so I advise you not to provoke them. Speaking to anyone about your situation, such as Police, F.B.I., etc., will result in your daughter being beheaded. If we catch you talking to a stray dog, she dies. If you alert bank authorities, she dies. If the money is in any way marked or tam-

pered with, she dies. You will be scanned for electronic devices and if any are found, she dies. You can try to deceive us but be warned that we are familiar with Law enforcement countermeasures and tactics. You stand a 99% chance of killing your daughter if you try to out smart us. Follow our instructions and you stand a 100% chance of getting her back. You and your family are under constant scrutiny as well as the authorities. Don't try to grow a brain, John. You are not the only fat cat around so don't think that killing will be difficult. Don't underestimate us John. Use that good southern common sense of yours. It is up to you now John!

Victory!
S.B.T.C.

I kneel on the floor trying to absorb the meaning of the handwritten, three-page ransom note. I scream at Patsy to call 911 as she is standing by the phone. It's a call that's been recorded and played many times over the Internet and on radio and TV. She's hysterical. She then calls our friends. "JonBenét's missing! Please, Come quick!"

I feel like I've been slugged in the stomach, and my mind is spinning. *I've got to get our baby back. Got to get her back. Get her back.* I try to think how I can get the money the kidnappers demanded in the note. I'm still in my underwear. I hurry upstairs to put some clothes on, and run back downstairs. Patsy rushes to check on Burke and he is still asleep. A lone policeman pulls up in front of our house, and I meet the uniformed officer in the front hallway. "Do you think she could have just run away?" he asks. I scoff, "*No*, she's only six years old." Our friends begin to arrive.

The officer reads the ransom note, asks more questions, and sequesters us in the sunroom. Our baby girl—kidnapped. We become concerned for Burke. He shouldn't wake up to all this confusion. We wake him and explain that JonBenét is missing and he'll be going to his friend's house for a little while.

"Will she come back?"

"Of course. Yes. We'll find her."

"And then we'll go on the plane?"

"Yes, then we'll go on the plane." He leaves with tears in his eyes and his new Nintendo 64 game under his arm. I want to run after him, hold him in my arms, not let him out of my sight.

Our priest from St. John's Episcopal Church, Rol Hoverstock, comes through the front door. An hour or so later a female detective arrives. The detective tells Patsy that kidnappers sometimes chicken out—drop the child off along the road or in a parking lot—so she should take heart. I'm searching for how someone got into our house. Which door? Which window? I call my banker in Atlanta to arrange for the ransom money. More squad cars arrive with police and phone monitoring equipment, and two women from the Boulder Police Department Victim's Advocate Unit. I call my copilot and ask him to try and contact Melinda and John Andrew, who are on a flight from Atlanta to Minneapolis. Our original plan was to rendezvous in Minneapolis and then go on to Charlevoix together in my plane. My banker calls, rankling the police because we're waiting for the kidnappers to call. My banker tells me they increased my Visa Card credit line so I could withdraw the $118,000 ransom money quickly. I can get the money as a cash advance.

Thank God. Now to wait for their call.

Call, you monsters, you inhuman beasts!
Just call.

I remember last summer when I got locked out of the house; I broke a pane in a basement window, reached in and pulled open the latch, and was able to climb inside. Patsy had asked our cleaning lady's husband to fix that window. Had it been fixed? I rush downstairs to check.

No.

The pane is still broken.

The window stands wide open.

A big old Samsonite suitcase is set beneath the window. Who put that there? The suitcase is like a stool to climb up and crawl out the window.

Where are you, JonBenét? Be brave, Johnnie Bee—We'll find you!

I rush up the stairs. I tell one of the policemen about the window. I can barely form the words. I'm sick to my stomach. I have to keep my wits about me. Patsy is in shock. She sits rocking and moaning, a mixing bowl between her knees as the urge to vomit is close. She's praying and clinging to a wooden cross that she had fashioned as part of the Christmas decorations in the sunroom. There's much turmoil. People milling about, talking, police coming and going. I tell myself, *Keep focused, John. JonBenét is depending on you now more than ever. You've got to stay strong. You've got to get your baby back.*

Where's the FBI? Shouldn't they be here by now? We need more help. Didn't the lady detective tell me they're on the way? Where are they? And what about that strange car across the street?

I don't realize that standard procedure when a child is missing is that the police do a thorough search of the entire house first in the event the child is playing, or hiding, or has fallen asleep somewhere other than her room. The police do not make that search.

They give me instructions for speaking with the kidnappers on the telephone. "Ask to talk to JonBenét. You must insist on hearing her voice."

"Okay, okay." I'm numb. My stomach is caved and knotted.

"Keep them on the line as long as you can. That's critical."

"Okay." The most important phone call of my life. I'm not sure I can do it right, but I must. "Okay."

Every time the phone rings, I jump. Patsy is on her knees clinging to the cross, moaning. One caller hangs up without saying anything. Was that the kidnapper?

I go into the kitchen, where a couple of officers are drinking coffee. Someone's making sandwiches. I stand staring out the kitchen window at our backyard, the empty trees dormant in the winter wind, the scrappy patches of browned grass dead and silent, Patsy's flower gardens now barren as though shrunken back into the bleakness of the earth. The children's slide and swing set look tired and abandoned. Our backyard we had so lovingly landscaped with colorful flowers, trees, and grass stares back at me with a hostile, frozen expression, as though announcing *we will never smile again.*

This is no longer winter's artistry. It's a world gone mad.

My body aches; my heart pounds so hard I can hear it. I try to breathe deep, but the air cobbles in my throat like flannel, and I don't feel like I can get enough air. A wave of fear overtakes me as I think of the possible reality that we won't get JonBenét back soon enough. The view from the window grows clouded, and a thick layer of gray film moves across the kitchen to the stainless steel sink, the Mexican tile countertops, Patsy's rooster paintings and collection of ceramic pitchers, the tile flooring. Tears sting my eyes. *Where is my little girl?*

My mind screams with one image alone, that my baby is out there unprotected and alone somewhere. It is cold. But she is strong. She knows I will find her. *JonBenét, JonBenét, JonBenét.* Police in uniforms with their leathery smells and dispassionate faces have invaded my house. I have to do something. I can't just wait. I have to do everything and anything I can to get my child back.

Someone has taken our child.

Can't anyone understand? Why isn't the entire town looking for my child, knocking down doors, shining high-powered spotlights into dark places? Why aren't they sending out bloodhounds, searching houses and back alleys, setting up roadblocks on the interstate?—MY GOD, OUR CHILD HAS BEEN KIDNAPPED!!!

The morning passes, grueling moment by moment.

Early afternoon.

No call from the kidnappers.

He's laughing at us. Somewhere right now the kidnapper is laughing at us.

Are there more than one? The ransom note says "we."

I look through the mail waiting on the floor beneath the mail slot in the front door, hoping there might be another communication from the kidnappers. Nothing but bills and Christmas cards. We are now almost insane with tension.

We're questioned for names of people we think might do this thing. Patsy remembers her cleaning lady telling her mother, "JonBenét is so pretty, aren't you afraid that someone might kidnap her?" Suddenly everyone seems suspicious. The minutes go by and we're getting desperate. I can smell the coffee brewing in the kitchen. Someone is preparing more food. I don't realize that everyone should have been made to stay in one particular area to keep us from contaminating potential evidence. Crime scene technicians are dusting for fingerprints. People are wandering all over the house.

Where is the FBI? Where are more police?

Patsy is surrounded by friends. Thank God. They're taking care of her. I'm trying to stay sane, trying to think logically. *What to do. What to do. I must DO something.*

Still no phone call.

The female detective asks me to take someone with me and go through the entire house to see if anything is unusual or out of place. Okay, sure. We decide to work from the bottom up since the third floor has no access to the outside. "Right. Basement first," and we head down the stairs. My legs are trembling and I stumble on the stair. I regain my balance. I head down the basement stairs and into the room where Burke's electric train is set up. I show my friend the broken window, which is still open, the small splinters of glass on the floor and on the suitcase. "This isn't right. The suitcase shouldn't be here." Did the kidnapper take my child out the basement window? My friend didn't tell me he had already noted the open window when he was down here earlier. I'm feeling dizzy.

Try to stay calm. Try to breathe. My friend says something but I can't hear him. I must find some clue to help me get my child back. We're supposed to be celebrating Christmas. We're supposed to be on our way to Michigan. This is our vacation, our family time!

I move down the hall to the door by the old steam boiler. I twist the latch and pull the door open. In the darkness I make out something there on the floor, a form. A white blanket, what—*what*—? I fumble to flip the light on. Little arms tied over her head. JonBenét! *I've found her!* My child, lying on the floor with a blanket over her. *Thank God, I've found her.* But her hands are bound together by a cord and there's black duct tape across her mouth. I don't see the garrote around her neck because it's so deeply embedded in her skin. I throw myself down on the floor over her body, and quickly pull the tape off her mouth. "Honey, it's okay. I'm here now. Daddy's here. Please say something, JonBenét!" Her face has a sweet look of peace, her eyes are closed, her skin cool. I felt a rush of relief and terror at the same time.

I try to untie her hands but I can't. The knot is too complicated. "JonBenét!" I hysterically pray she is just unconscious.

I lift my little girl up from beneath her arms. Her body is stiff and cool. The last time I carried her she was sound asleep, her warm breath on my neck. I scream like a madman. I can't form words. I can only scream. Scream and scream.

I carry my baby up the basement stairs, rush into the living room with her, and lay her down on the rug in front of the Christmas tree. I've got to wake her up. Keep her breathing! Help, someone! *Call an ambulance!*

I hug my child's stiff body. I kiss her chilled cheeks. *Do something! Somebody do something!*

Patsy's friends are trying to hold her back from seeing JonBenét like this, but she fights her way through them screaming. She rushes for her child, falls on her body shrieking.

The female detective feels for a pulse and looks me in the eyes and says, "She's dead."

My heart stops.

Father Rol starts to pray. He's praying the Episcopal Last Rites.

Patsy sobs, "Pray to raise her from the dead! Like Lazarus! Pray to raise her!"

Father Rol reaches for Patsy, puts his arms around her to comfort her. I can't move. He's praying the Lord's Prayer.

My body feels like it's cast in stone. I can't breathe. *Patsy, Patsy, our baby is gone.*

CHAPTER 2

Messages from Heaven

*Oh, that my grief were fully weighed,
And my calamity laid with it on the scales!
For then it would be heavier than the sand
of the sea—*

—Job 6:2–3

The coroner's autopsy disclosed that not only had JonBenét been strangled, but her skull had been fractured by an enormous blow, which had gone unnoticed at first. The garrote around her neck had strangled her, and so when given the blow to the head, she was already dead and didn't bleed. Officially, her death was caused by asphyxia due to strangulation associated with massive head trauma.

We could not bear to hear these details and refused to read the report. We still couldn't grasp that our little girl had been murdered. That's the dreadful news you read about in the papers or hear on the nightly news of *other* people's children—certainly not your own.

When they pronounced our child dead, Patsy's shrieks were so horrible they surely had to be heard and recorded in Heaven and earth's archives of parental anguish. Her daughter lay murdered on the floor before the Christmas tree she had gazed at with anticipation just the day before. Patsy has lost her only daughter. Our baby. Our joy and our delight.

The Boulder police ushered us out of our home. Agonized and in shock, we didn't know what to do or where to go. My children from my first marriage, John Andrew and Melinda, had quickly boarded a flight from Minneapolis to Denver when they found out what was happening. They arrived in a taxicab just as we were being escorted out of our house. I hugged them and then had to tell them that their little sister, JonBenét, was gone.

Friends offered to take us in, and the police descended on their house soon after we arrived. I thought they were there to protect us. I realized later they were probably there to observe us. The next day people started to arrive: my brother, Jeff; Patsy's sister Pam; and friends from Atlanta, the city we had always considered our hometown. We were surrounded by family and friends, all of us stunned and desolate. Patsy was senseless in shock. When I tried to speak to her, hold her, she collapsed against me, unable to lift her body up, producing horrible guttural moans like a woman in labor. "Who would *do* this? Why? Who would *do* this to my baby?"

Patsy's friends steadied her to keep her from collapsing to the floor, and then helped her onto a bed. We left our home without so much as a toothbrush or a comb. Our physician was called and he prescribed medication for us. My host poured Scotch, but no medication or drink could take away the horror of what happened to our JonBenét.

The police remained with us, watching us, questioning our friends and family. There was no way to sleep and no way to stay alert.

Days went by and Patsy's sister Pam suggested she drive over to our house on University Hill and pack up some clothes and necessary items for us. It took a while to get permission, but the police finally gave their consent for her to gather some of our things, but only under their watchful eye. Pam drove to our darkened house on 15th Street, a house we would never again step foot into. Along the sidewalk were the tokens of sympathy from the people of Boulder: bouquets of flowers, teddy bears, little angels, cards, and placards, *"We will miss you, JonBenét."* Yellow police tape had been draped across the lawn, Patsy's red-and-white-striped candy canes were still planted along each side of the entry walk, paper bag luminaries sat on the brown grass, and a toy Santa in his sleigh lay tipped over on its side as though in mourning. Christmas wreaths still decorated the windows and doors.

Pam entered the single solid oak front door, passed through the foyer, the hallway, and past our now desolate Christmas tree. She climbed the front stairs to our bedroom on the third floor and stood staring at the darkened, empty room, the bed still unmade. *Shouldn't they still be there somewhere? Shouldn't Patsy be just over there in her bathroom brushing her teeth maybe? And John putting on his jacket making plans for the day?* She could feel our presence in the room that we had lovingly remodeled and created as our own little haven, and she felt nauseous. *This is a nightmare. I'm dreaming. This can't be real.* Under the glare of a Boulder police officer, she began gathering clothes from our closets. Shirts, jackets, pants, underwear, Patsy's hair dryer, my electric razor. *What else? Patsy's favorite earrings? Her wedding pictures? My God, what to pack?* In a wildfire, what do you grab before the flames engulf your house? The officer seemed impatient and made a comment about parents who murder their children. *What did he mean by that?*

Shaking, she headed down the stairs to the second floor. The children's floor. First, Burke's room. She wanted to take down the model airplane hanging from his ceiling, but the officer stopped her, ordering her to hurry up and take only what was necessary. *Burke's jeans, tennis shoes, shirts, what about his toys? His Christmas presents? Oh God, she must be dreaming. Sweet little Burke, how was he taking all this? His mittens, his model airplanes, his basketball.* His comfy boy's room he'd never see again. But wait, there was one more room she had to visit. She left Burke's room and walked through the playroom with the cabinets of toys, the big beanbag chair, JonBenét's trunk of costumes and dress-up clothes. Burke's collection of trucks and airplanes was there just like always. Pam wanted to stay in the playroom, wait for Burke and JonBenét to come running in, pull out a book to read to them, Dr. Seuss maybe, but with the police officer behind her, she kept moving, through the hall, past the upstairs laundry area, toward John Andrew's room. She made an abrupt stop at JonBenét's door. She pushed back a sob as she peered inside at the sight of the Christmas tree decorated with dozens of sparkling angels and snowflakes, and then quickly stepped under the police tape into the room. *Johnnie Bee's Christmas room, my God, look at this display of love Patsy invested in these kids. Burke's room is all boy, blue, red, and white and filled with boy stuff—but this room, this room is the domain of a fairy princess.* She brushed her hand across JonBenét's bedpost, her only niece's twin bed, the peach-colored sheets still rumpled from where she had been taken. Here were her dolls, her toys, her shelves of picture books and Bible stories, the hand-carved corner hutch with her decorated bicycle contest blue ribbon from last summer and other pageant awards. Here were the lovely paisley drapes Patsy had specially selected so they'd be just right for the room. Here were the doors to her balcony, where JonBenét could play Juliet or Rapunzel, or carry all her dolls and stuffed animals outside to perform for them. Pam could see her little niece playing on the soft carpet with her dolls, happily chattering all the voices for each one, her little pink sneakers with the pom-pom laces kicked to the corner, the dollhouse and its tiny figures spread out. She could feel JonBenét's presence, her exuberance. The closet door ajar, her clothes and toys lying in disarray inside, a tap shoe lying upside down as though just tossed from a little foot after a rehearsal. Pam bent to pick it up when a policeman barked at her not to touch. She started to leave the room but felt compelled to take a small medal about the size of a silver dollar from a shelf of JonBenét's trophies.

She returned to the house where we were staying, and opened her palm to show me the medal. "I don't know why, John, but I just had a strong impression I was supposed to bring this medal to you." I saw the medal and began to sob uncontrollably. Of all the mementos Pam could have chosen to give me, she chose the one most precious of all to me. Pam couldn't have known it, but it was the medal JonBenét had wanted me, her dad, to have. The one she placed around my neck and said, "This is for you, Daddy. I won it for you."

That was five days before Christmas.

It was as if JonBenét were speaking to me from Heaven and telling me, "Daddy, I'm all right. Here, this is for you. Remember? I won it for you." I knew it was a gift from God to a broken father.

I wore this priceless medal around my neck twenty-four hours a day for a year until the eyelet on top wore through and the ribbon frayed to threads. I carry it in my wallet to this day. It reminds me, "Daddy, I'm all right." Our JonBenét is with God in Heaven and she's all right. If I doubt that, all I have to do is pull the small medal out and hold it in my hand. She's with God in Heaven and she's all right.

It's years later now, and I've come to a place where small things are significant to me. For so many years of my life it was the big things that counted: houses, cars, boats, planes. Patsy loved to host dinner parties; the more people, the merrier.

In those high-flying days I never dreamed that one day I would downsize to the point of selling most of the treasures we owned, and that I would be calling a boat my home. I never dreamed, with a master's degree and many years as a successful businessman with seven hundred employees, that I'd wind up jobless.

An ideal Christmas, that Christmas of 1996.

I wandered around the home of our gracious friends in the wee hours in stocking feet. I came across their cache of Christmas cards on the mantel in their family room. Happy, loving wishes from so many people. I spotted our Christmas letter, the one Patsy had composed early in December. She had labored at it, wondering what to leave out. So much good in our lives to report. My heart beat in my ears as I read:

Dear Friends and Family,
  It's been another busy year at the Ramsey

household. Can't believe it's almost over and time to start again!

Melinda has graduated from the Medical College of Georgia and is working in Pediatrics ICU at Kennestone Hospital in Atlanta. John Andrew (2nd) is a sophomore at the University of Colorado.

Burke is a busy fourth grader where he really shines in math and spelling. He played flag football this fall and is currently on a basketball binge! His little league team was #1. He's lost just about all of his baby teeth, so I'm sure we'll be seeing the orthodontist in 1997!

JonBenét is enjoying her first year in "real school." Kindergarten in the Core Knowledge program is fast paced and five full days a week. She has already been moved ahead to first grade math. She continues to enjoy participating in talent and modeling pageants. She was named "America's Royale Tiny Miss" last summer and is Colorado's Little Miss Christmas. Her teacher says she is so outgoing that she will never have trouble delivering an oral book report!

John is always on the go traveling hither and yon. Access recently celebrated its one billion $$ mark in sales, so he's pretty happy! He and his crew were underway in the Port Huron to

Mackinac Island yacht race in July, but had to pull out midway due to lack of wind. (Can you believe that?) But, his real love is the new "old looking" boat, Grand Season, which he spent months designing.

I spend most of my "free time" working at the school and doing volunteer work. The Charlevoix house was on the home tour in July and will likely appear in one of the Better Homes and Gardens publications in 1997. On a recent trip to NYC, my friend and I appeared amid the throng of fans on the TODAY show. Al Roker and Bryant actually talked to us and we were on camera for a few fleeting moments!

We are all enjoying continued good health and look forward to seeing you in 1997! One final note... thank you to all my "friends" and my dear husband for surprising me with the biggest, most outrageous 40th birthday bash I've ever had! We'll be spending my actual birthday on the Disney Big Red Boat over the New Year!

Merry Christmas and much love,

The Ramseys

The madness had just begun. The day after the murder of our child, Patsy and I sat frozen in grief surrounded by friends and family, Patsy nearly comatose, unable to stand up or feed herself. Our host approached me where I sat slumped on the sofa staring at the floor.

"There's someone on the phone, John, from your office. He says it's important. Do you want to take it?"

I recognized the name.

"He's quite insistent, John."

I reached for the receiver.

"John?"

"Yes...this is John."

"I'm sorry to bother you but I was told to get you this message: John, the police are out to get you."

"*What?*"

"The police think you murdered JonBenét."

"*What?* That's insane."

"John, let me finish. I received a call from inside the system, I can't tell you who it was, but the person told me to get this message to you as soon as possible. He said specifically, 'Tell John to get the best defense attorney he can get his hands on. The Boulder police think he killed his daughter.'"

"*What?*"

"And they're out to get you."

"I don't believe it. No one could think such a thing—No! I can't believe—"

"John, that is the message I was given. The person is reliable who passed this on to me. I'm so sorry to have to give you news like this."

Oh my God.

I held on to the phone staring at it in disbelief. Our hearts and lives had been shattered with the loss of our baby, our beloved child. Police *out to get me?*

The caller proved to be right. We didn't think it was possible; it was, after all, unthinkable that we would so much as lift a finger to hurt our child. I had never, ever, even spanked her. I never spanked or physically disciplined any of my children. I didn't need to. A stern word from me, a serious look, and that's all it took. But to our shock and dismay, the police focused on Patsy and me, putting us under "the umbrella of suspicion," a term they invented when they announced their thoughts to the media. As the police focused solely on Patsy and me, the media were in lockstep with the police, anxious for all the juicy details, and eager to serve us up for execution. The police didn't disappoint them. What a story it made. They labeled our girl a child beauty queen, and drummed up all sort of macabre stories about our family and home. (Years later we filed six lawsuits against the tabloids and reached settlements, but these victories went unpublicized.) Suspicion was cast. Our name and integrity would fast be destroyed. We were to become targets in the giant labyrinth of an international media frenzy that would be still alive almost twenty years later.

"John, how could they do this to us?" Patsy wailed, agonized. "Why? Why?"

The police were hungry for evidence to indict us for murder, any kind of evidence. They had made their decision, now they just needed to find evidence to back it up. As the days went on, the police shifted their focus from me to Patsy. JonBenét occasionally wet the bed and they decided this could be what had precipitated murder. The police theorized that Patsy, on a peaceful Christmas night after preparing, shopping, baking, decorating, and planning our family Christmas and Disney cruise for weeks, had gone into a rage because her little girl *may* have wet the bed. They suspected Patsy of a vicious and sick murder because her child *may* have wet the bed. What mother who had survived the horrors of ovarian cancer would murder the pride and joy of her life, her baby—for a thing like wetting the bed? The very thought shocked us and horrified everyone who knew our family. It was lunacy.

Unknown to us, the media were being stoked by police misinformation, leaks, and innuendos. Their strategy for solving the case was to bring such intense pressure on us that one of us would crack and confess. We soon became international news. I was confused and angry. Why were all these lies being said about me and my family? Our child's picture was on the cover of every tabloid in the world. Patsy and I both were branded as murderers. Though never officially called suspects by the police, and without the smallest shred of evidence, the media and popular opinion were being manipulated by the police to convict us in the court of public opinion.

CHAPTER 3

Why Suffering?

If we learn from suffering, then all the world should be wise, since all suffer.
—Anne Morrow Lindberg

I walk into the freedom of the outdoors and wish it could be just that, free—a web of poplars, a ray of sun slanting through the leaves, the smell of earth relieved of winter, a bird singing; I wish I could scroll back just for a moment, one moment with my children giggling and chattering at my side in the breeze of an early spring with new roots of grass and yellow forsythia buds surfacing. I realize as my heart pounds against my shirt that no walk outside will be easy now. I spot the TV truck at the curb behind the buckthorn bushes; my jaw clenches at the sight of the nest of reporters. Do any of them have children? I wonder. The reporter who posed as a telephone repairman, fiddling with the wires at the side of the house to gain access to our private conversations, did he have children? Does anyone call him Daddy when he returns home from work after masquerading as something he is not?

I'd like to go back and sit on my children's swing and scrape my feet on the sand worn concave by little sneakers. I remember JonBenét's sneakers with the butterflies on the toes. "Look, Daddy, see my new shoes!"

Ever since she was an infant, she loved anything that sparkled or lit up. She clapped her hands with delight at our first Christmas tree and the colored lights. JonBenét had been operating with her throttle wide open ever since her birth. She was born at Northside Hospital in Atlanta, Georgia, exactly thirty-two minutes after Patsy woke me up and said, "John, it's time. We've got to leave for the hospital now!" To say JonBenét arrived on this earth with enthusiasm would be an understatement.

You laughed with your children and marveled at their innocence and curiosity. Now, face it. You'll never be happy again. And maybe you'll never again see light, not the kind you had always defined as bright or beautiful, no, you'd never find that again.

Had we been a praying family? Yes, sure, we prayed. Always when we needed help from God. We bowed our heads before meals, sometimes. We thanked God for all our blessings, sometimes. Patsy and I always kissed our children at bedtime, always told them we loved them, and sometimes said their bedtime prayers with them. "Now I lay me down to sleep..." We prayed in church. But I asked myself, why didn't I pray more? What did I do wrong? Where had I fallen short in God's eyes? Why didn't He protect JonBenét? Was I being punished by God? Surely not. God wouldn't take my child from me to punish me. In my immature faith I couldn't imagine what I might have done that God would punish me this way.

I blamed myself for what happened. How could I *not* blame myself? I didn't make sure our home was secure. I never imagined it would be invaded while we slept. Patsy and I wracked our brains, hammered our heads and hearts with so many questions. Why did we not see how vulnerable a child in pageants might be? Why didn't I have that home alarm fixed? Why didn't I check to see that the window in our basement was fixed? Why did we permit our home to be open for the public to stroll through for the historic home tour? Why did we host a church Christmas party and permit all those strangers into our home? Why didn't I wait to deliver the dog to our neighbors to dog-sit until just before we left? Why did I allow our company's successes to be reported in the newspaper? Why did we think we were safe and impervious to evil? Why why why? It was tormenting to know I couldn't undo the past, couldn't turn back the clock and do things differently. I also accused God. *Where were you, God? Why didn't you stop this killer? Why didn't you save our child?*

Why didn't *I* save my child?

When things go wrong, the tendency is to blame God first. He let me down, He didn't protect me. Then we often blame others. It's someone else's fault. And lastly we fix blame on ourselves. God never pointed a cruel accusative finger at Patsy and me. It couldn't be God who rained curses down on us. So we knew we had to stop blaming Him for failing us, but I couldn't help but scream, "Where were you, God? Why did you let this happen?"

I had to stop making God the scapegoat, or the cause of our tragedy, failing to be there when

JonBenét needed Him. People often say, God won't give you any more than you can handle. It seemed to me He gave JonBenét more than she could handle that night. I had a long way to go to understand what God promises us and what He doesn't promise us.

A reporter asked Patsy, "Mrs. Ramsey, how have you held up during all this for so long?" Patsy, eyes flashing, responded, "I believe in God," she said, "and my faith in God has sustained me. Period. *I trust Him.*"

The most common question most of us ask when the storms of life come at us unexpectedly, and through no apparent fault of our own, and when life treats us unfairly is, "Why?" *Why* did this happen?

I asked *Why?* when my oldest daughter, Beth, was killed in a car accident. I certainly asked *Why?* when JonBenét was taken from us, and when the Boulder police focused on Patsy and me as her murderer, I wanted to know *Why?*

When we ask God the question *Why?*, it is really not a question, it's an accusation. We, in a sense, are accusing God of causing the disaster, and we're saying to Him, "Why did *You* do this? Why did *You* allow this to happen?"

Suffering and tragedy are perhaps the biggest reason people give up on God. When tragedy strikes, our faith changes. Faith cannot stay the same after tragedy because it has been challenged. It either diminishes or deepens. I heard a sermon that stated, "You can be broken, bitter, barren, or better as a result of suffering." I was at the broken stage because my faith had struck rock bottom in 1992 when Beth was killed. She was a beautiful twenty-two-year-old young woman, six months out of college. Now JonBenét was gone, too, and I plummeted into a well of despair from which I wasn't sure I would return. The word I repeated over and over was the desperate and accusatory *Why?*

I think now, suppose God bent down and answered my *Why*'s with holy, perfect reasons. Would I be satisfied with His answers? Of course not. I wanted my daughters back. I just wanted my daughters back.

Do you know anyone who has *not* asked God *Why?* at some point in their life? It's natural and normal to ask that question when tragedy strikes. We want to figure things out, understand, gain some sense of comprehending the reasoning behind what we find so unreasonable, unfair, and unthinkable. Over the centuries the acumen of humankind has come up with enormous progress, multitudes of important discoveries and advancements, but the question *Why human suffering?* remains unanswered for even the greatest thinkers.

I remember a high school teacher admonishing us after the whole class complained about an unfair exam, by simply stating, "Look. Life is not fair—get used to it!" We didn't think it was amusing at the time, but how right she was. I've learned to accept that axiom of truth and I've added one more: Life is not easy. These two truths are simple facts of life:

Life is not always fair.

Life is not always easy.

Fairness is another word for justice. Nothing makes us more upset than to be treated unjustly. If something is unfair, we want something done about it. I read recently that there are a hundred million lawsuits in the U.S. court system at any given time. All of these lawsuits are filed because of alleged *injustice.* When we were children, our parents or teachers were the administrators of justice. But what happens when our parents or teachers aren't around and we are out in the harsh world? What happens then? We're frustrated, feel cheated, and are angry. It's not *fair.*

More than a billion people don't have enough to eat every day. More than a hundred million people died due to war or genocide in the twentieth century. Crime and poverty rates are climbing worldwide. And we will never get over 9/11 when the World Trade Center was struck by Islamic fanatics and nearly three thousand innocent lives were lost.

Up to my thirties, I was under the misconception that life was supposed to be comfortable, that we were meant to be free from pain and suffering. When life wasn't easy for me, I thought I was the oddball. It seemed like life was easy for those around me. I just didn't see their burdens. Not until I was struck myself and my eyes were opened to the suffering of others did I understand that almost everyone carries pain of some sort.

Some people carry impossible burdens, and yet they go on. How do they do it?

CHAPTER 4

Life in Chaos

*God whispers to us in our pleasures,
Speaks in our conscience,
But shouts in our pain;
It is His megaphone to rouse a deaf world.*
—C. S. Lewis

I had always been a man who could control his emotions. I almost never, ever had angry outbursts. I didn't cry at a sad book or movie. I wasn't given to argumentativeness. I was a compromiser. It wasn't in my nature to shout or fight, or conversely, get overly excited. *Newsweek* magazine labeled me phlegmatic. (I had to look the word up to see if that was a good thing or a bad thing.) I'd never really been one to express my emotions in any demonstrative manner, but when I lost my daughters, I wept constantly. After JonBenét died, we wanted to leave Boulder and go back home, back home to Atlanta. We had lived in Atlanta for many years; Burke, JonBenét, and John Andrew were born there, and our families and lifelong friends were there. Beth was buried there, and now JonBenét would be buried next to her.

As I made preparations for JonBenét's funeral, my good friend Mike Bynum learned that the police refused to release JonBenét's body for the service. The police were adamant about interrogating us more before they would release her body. Mike was furious and contacted the district attorney's office, insisting the DA get involved. The district attorney challenged the police and informed them it was unlawful to hold a body for no cause or purpose. The police relented and let us take our little girl back to Atlanta to bury her. Mike did not tell us about this confrontation with the police until after the funeral. He knew it would be terribly upsetting to us, but decided to tell us about it so we would understand who we were dealing with in the Boulder police.

In a show of compassion, our parent company, Lockheed Martin, sent a private plane and pilot to fly us back to Atlanta. It was a gift of thoughtfulness that allowed us to avoid the media swarm that was growing around us like flies. Lockheed Martin would go on to show a level of caring well beyond what would be expected from a large megacorporation.

Dr. Frank Harrington, senior minister of the Peachtree Presbyterian Church in Atlanta, who married Patsy and me and baptized Burke and JonBenét, would preside over the funeral. He embraced me in the back room before the service and said, "John, I promise you the memories that bring tears today will bring smiles tomorrow." At that point I couldn't imagine the memory of JonBenét bringing anything but tears. What was there to smile about when my six-year-old lay dead in a casket a few feet away? Where was God?

Patsy said that morning, "If there's any more suffering ahead for me, I don't know if I will be able to endure it." Of course there was suffering ahead, and we both knew it.

"We will endure, darling," I promised her.

I took both her hands in mine and I said nothing more. We remained in silence for a while, Patsy barely able to stand up, and then we entered the sanctuary with our family. I put my arm around her so she wouldn't stumble, and together we took our seats in the front row to say good-bye to our daughter.

The church was decorated for Christmas, for happy times. Banks of poinsettias and ribboned garlands lined the walls. JonBenét lay in an open casket festooned with flowers. On her head was the "Little Miss Christmas" tiara that she had won just days before. She held a gold cross from Patsy, a gold bracelet from her grandma, and her gray and white stuffed cat she had named "Sister Socks" under her right arm. I gently tucked my favorite silk scarf beside her left arm. The lid of the casket was closed with pools of roses dripping over its edges. How forever sad the world would be without the sounds and life of this vibrant child.

After the service we walked out the front doors of the church to take our place in the funeral procession, and immediately were jolted from grief to shock as cameramen and reporters appeared from behind every pillar and bush. They jostled with each other to snap photographs of us getting into the limousine; they photographed us struggling for composure; they photographed our child's casket being carried by the pallbearers. When we arrived at the cemetery, reporters and cameramen tried to pry their way in for photos of the graveside service. We were only vaguely aware what was happening, or the firestorm that was igniting around us. The media were ravenous for another sensational story to fill talk show banter and lurid headlines since the O. J. Simpson trial had just ended. Our family tragedy quickly fed that insatiable hunger, and this media feeding frenzy would continue for years. I stood at our baby's graveside remembering the day we'd buried Beth in the same place, four years earlier. Nothing made sense.

We laid JonBenét to rest in Atlanta, and within a few days made the dreaded trip back to Boulder. I was eager to help the police find our child's killer, and Patsy felt it would be best for Burke to finish his school year with his friends at High Peaks Elementary School. We knew the police were squarely focused on Patsy and me as their only suspects, but we assumed they would quickly realize we were loving parents not capable of such a horrible act.

There was the matter of the ransom note. The police asked us to give handwriting samples so handwriting experts could analyze and compare them with the writing of the ransom note. "Whatever for?" Patsy wondered, but we complied. Not once, but several times we were required to copy word-for-word the ransom note in our own writing, first with our right hand, and then with our left. Patsy would burst into sobs at the words such as, "...*result in your daughter being beheaded...*" Our efforts, every step we took, every move we made to do what we thought was right, did little to quiet the media's firestorm of accusations.

Between January and April 1997, Patsy gave five

extensive handwriting samples. She was exhausted and we were beginning to get the picture. The police were trying to prove that Patsy had written the three-page ransom note.

We couldn't comprehend such an idea. Patsy agonized over and over again, "Oh, John, what have I ever done to give anyone the idea that I could kill my baby?"

Some seasoned investigators outside of the Boulder Police Department believed JonBenét's murder was a kidnapping gone wrong. Others believed the killer was a demented pedophile. In searching for information, I learned that pedophiles typically take a child, molest them, and then let them go. To me, the ransom note read like the ramblings of a very unstable young person with a disgusting, sick mind and imagination influenced by crime movies. Still, the police focused all their suspicion on Patsy and me. From the very beginning, police psychologists advised the detectives that the ransom note was not the kind of note a parent would write. All the credible experts assessed the likelihood of either of us being the author of this note to be nil. The Secret Service handwriting experts concluded that neither Patsy nor I had written the note. That didn't seem to deter the police away from their quick conclusion that we were guilty. A veteran district attorney told me, "There is nothing more dangerous in this country than a police department that has made up its mind." The police department had made up its mind on day one and were not about to be swayed by facts or evidence. Police are supposed to investigate a crime and turn the results of the investigation over to the prosecuting attorney. They are not empowered to determine guilt or innocence.

Because a pubic hair was found on the blanket covering JonBenét's body, police subjected us to the most humiliating and embarrassing of procedures. On an icy February morning a friend drove us to the Boulder Community Hospital to have pubic hair taken for comparison and testing. We were mortified. We were taken to separate examination rooms and told to disrobe and lie down on a table for the examination. Two detectives stood alongside watching as the nurse combed the pubic hair, transferring a sample to an envelope. Snipping away, she gave the envelope to the officers. I bit my lip and went through it, but it made me angry to think that Patsy was forced to endure the same humiliating process in another room. This was to be the beginning of a total assault on our privacy and personal lives.

Patsy told me later she had burst into sobs because the nurse was wearing a pink sweatshirt with red hearts like the ones she and JonBenét used to make with puffy pens for Valentine's Day.

"Can we please get out of here now?"

"Yes, we're finished."

Finished.

There was no match.

Now we had given saliva, fingerprints, palm prints, handprints, blood samples, hair samples, pubic hair samples, and handwriting samples. Weren't these enough to satisfy the police suspicions and convince them that we were innocent?

Enhanced photos of JonBenét were splashed on newsstands and television screens around the world. The newspaper and magazine art departments added lipstick, rouge, eye shadow, and liner to some of JonBenét's photos to make her look more made-up. That wasn't our sweet, innocent child. Personal photos of our family appeared in print without our authorization. A professional photographer in Charlevoix whom we hired to take our family's photos for our Christmas cards sold the pictures to the highest tabloid bidder. Other photographs of ours that we had sent for developing earlier were stolen and sold as well. JonBenét's medical records were stolen from her doctor's office files. The police crime scene photos were stolen and sold to the tabloids. I was horrified when JonBenét's autopsy photos ended up in the *Globe*. The videos of the pageants taken by the pageant promoters were sold to anybody who wanted to exploit our daughter, and the Internet became glutted with JonBenét videos, some with seductive, suggestive music.

A University of Colorado student put up an exhibit of JonBenét's pictures in the student center entitled "Daddy's Little Whore." Some other students tore the display down, and there was a big discussion in the media about free speech. I wrote the student a letter and suggested to him that when he had children of his own, he would understand the hurt he inflicted. JonBenét was an innocent six-year-old child full of personality and energy. Our normal, loving family was under cruel and vicious assault from all sides and a pattern began to emerge. The police were giving the media misleading information behind closed doors to fuel this assault.

I vowed I would spend every dime I had to find the killer of my daughter. I asked my attorney to bring in experienced investigators to find the madman who did this to my child. I would spend hundreds of thousands of dollars on lawyers and investigators because money didn't mean a thing to me anymore. Patsy often cried in her grief that she would gladly have traded places with JonBenét. "Why didn't they kill me instead?" she wept. I, too, would have laid down my life for my child in an instant. I regretted I couldn't have done just that.

CHAPTER 5

Angels

*And the LORD, He is the One who goes before you.
He will be with you,
He will not leave you nor forsake you;
do not fear nor be dismayed.*
—Deuteronomy 31:8

I took a walk in the rain by myself one afternoon after meeting with my lawyer, Lin Wood, in downtown Atlanta. It was 2001, and by now we had begun to file lawsuits against the tabloids for the slander and lies they had printed about our family. It felt good to hit back finally. As I walked, I saw a man wearing a worn miner's jacket and shabby boots sitting against the brick wall of a commercial building, a shopping cart parked beside him loaded with folded old blankets, pieces of cardboard, and bulging plastic sacks. I drew nearer, rain sliding down my face, my feet cold and wet, and he asked me if I could spare any change. I stopped, reached in my pocket, pulled out a crumpled five-dollar bill. He reached out his hand and gave me the perfunctory panhandler blessing, and I resumed my walk. A few steps away, I stopped and turned to him sitting there crouched against the wall with rain falling all around him on the pavement, thinking tonight he'd probably sleep on cardboard with one of those blankets wrapped around his legs.

I walked back to him, asked, "How did you become homeless?"

He looked up at me with an indignant air. "I'm not homeless, sir," he said heatedly. *"I'm just houseless."*

My God, my God, how quickly our comforts can be taken from us, how fast we can lose them all. Wasn't it just this morning I woke up as president of a thriving company, two nice cars in the garage, a boat in the marina, an airplane in the hangar? Wasn't it just this morning we were all alive and enjoying breakfast in our home on 15th Street on University Hill in Boulder, Colorado? Maybe this guy crouched on the pavement had a family. Maybe this guy had owned a business once with a luxury car in the garage, a little white Bichon Frise dog. What had brought him down? I wondered. Wasn't it just a few hours ago I'd sat at the table with my family, Burke asking for "more juice, please," helping Johnnie Bee open the lid of a fresh jar of peanut butter, and didn't I just tell her to please eat the crusts of her toast?

"But, Daddy, I don't like crusts."

Weren't we laughing together and looking forward to the day ahead? Thankfully I'd not fallen as far as this man. Fallen, yes, but still not homeless on a busy Atlanta street corner.

I started to appreciate the small things more and more. Those little hidden treasures waiting to be noticed, the small things that would bring a smile. I forced myself to "count my blessings." It's a clichéd phrase, I know, but those little gifts are there if I'd take a moment to recognize them. Small things like toast and peanut butter with the people you love—things like a medal no bigger than a silver dollar proudly given to her dad by a child. It's taken hardship and suffering for me to appreciate that it's the small things in life that give us a connection to God's world, and help to move our perspective beyond man's world. It can be in the smallest of things we can see Him.

I wondered how people heard the voice of God. Was it loud and clear? God spoke to the prophet, Elijah, in a still, *small* voice. I asked God in desperation, please speak to me. Please, Lord, guide my steps and show me my path.

Despite my beginning to better understand God, I was still forced to deal with life in the real world. The killer of my daughter was out there. Somewhere he was out there living, watching, waiting. If only the police would get beyond their fixation on us and look for the real killer.

We wanted to do whatever we could to find the killer of our daughter, so we took out newspaper ads offering a reward for any information about JonBenét's murder. We interviewed with Barbara Walters and made appearances on *Larry King Live*, *CNN Early Prime*, and other internationally broadcast programs. We wanted to keep the pressure on the police to do the right thing and not just throw our daughter's murder in a cold case file. Our real priority was to get the case moved from the Boulder police to another jurisdiction. Any other jurisdiction would be better. We believed that until a competent authority took over, the murder would never be solved. We learned that the Boulder police rarely followed up on any of the hundreds of leads that came into their department. Even the district attorney asked our private investigators to follow up on a lead he had received perhaps because he knew the police would not.

If no one in the police department believed we

were innocent, many other people did believe in us. Many people reached out to us with compassion and kindness. Strangers would frequently come up to us on the street or in restaurants. "I'm so sorry about what is being done to you and your family." "We believe in you." We received hundreds of encouraging letters! I was grateful for each letter and the thoughts they expressed and I tried to answer every one of them. One mother wrote, "Because of your story, I will now take that extra five minutes when my six-year-old daughter asks me to sit down and play teatime with her." The woman went on to say that she worked a full-time job and rarely had quality time to spend with her daughter, but she would now make that time. The letter, and others like it, made me think that good might actually come from JonBenét's short life on earth. I had always been self-focused with not much concern for my fellow man, but this outpouring of compassion from total strangers would change me forever.

John Douglas, the noted FBI profiler, told me that most victims of violent crime eventually end up broke. Dealing with the justice system, legal fees, making bad decisions under severe stress, lack of focus and motivation can be devastating financially. I was beginning to worry that we would end up broke, too. The media accused me of being cold, aloof, unfeeling, but inside I was simply heartbroken and sad. Our little daughter was gone.

I read that one of the policemen who came to our house on December twenty-sixth saw Patsy crying "through splayed fingers." The cops thought she looked suspicious and that she was faking her misery. It was also deemed suspicious that I paced while waiting for the supposed kidnappers to call. It was accusations like these that baffled me. Was there a manual of rules for parents on how to act when a child is missing or murdered? The entire police case against us was based on their sole conclusion that "we didn't act right." That was a questionable assessment coming from a police department who had never investigated this type of crime before.

Patsy often took the lead in praying. One early evening before falling asleep, Patsy said to me, "God won't fail us, He hasn't abandoned us, and He won't fail us, John."

"Yes, I know. I don't understand any of this, but if God is with us, I guess we can get through it," I said, looking at her drawn face.

"We've got to be strong—for our living children's

sake," she said. "Besides, JonBenét would not want her mom and dad to be sad."

"You're right," I said. I gave Patsy a hug and we fell into the peace we ached for sleep to bring.

We left our Boulder house on the afternoon of December twenty-sixth, 1996, never to return. For the next six months we moved from one friend's house to another, and it never took long for the media cameras to find us. We thanked God for the dear people who reached out to us with such loving kindness because by doing so their own privacy and peace were put in jeopardy. Imagine having houseguests who drew TV satellite trucks and dozens of photographers outside your front door twenty-four hours a day. It was hard on their lawns, for sure, not to mention their peace of mind. One of our hosts was chief financial officer for the University of Colorado and came under fire for harboring us in his home. A Denver radio talk show host demanded the removal of our friend from his university job because he gave us refuge. We were constantly hounded by tabloid photographers. The tabloids needed only an unusual photograph to fabricate a story around. It's called "tabloid magic." The photographers would taunt us to try and get a reaction because it would make a more sensational photo. The tabloids figured out that sensationalism sells, so rather than wait for something sensational to happen, they just made it up. They pay out millions every year in libel and slander suits but keep that fact confidential so they won't lose advertisers and readers.

One friend we stayed with got so angry and frustrated when a guy posing as a telephone repairman tried to tap his phone that he ran out of the house to run off the photographers who had gathered in a nearby empty lot. He carried a baseball bat for effect, which of course, was a bad idea. A few of the photographers quickly armed themselves with metal pipes, but before any damage to either side was done, the police showed up. Our poor friend was arrested and hauled off to jail. Patsy drove to the police station with her attorney to plead for his release. In tears, she reminded the police that someone had broken into our house and killed our little girl. "We're being positively hounded to death by photographers and reporters and TV cameras. Can't you do something to protect us?"

Our friend received a misdemeanor menace charge and now a good man had a police record. The killer's poison was spreading to those around us.

How far would it spread?

We had been accused by the media of not cooperating with the police, in spite of interminable interrogations, providing hundreds of personal records including our bills and household records, and giving permission to the police to scour our home, inch by inch, for as long as they chose. I wrote a letter to the district attorney dated April 11, 1998, to emphasize our desperate desire to work to find the killer of our child.

Here's the letter:

April 11, 1998

Dear Mr. Hunter:

I am writing this letter because it seems difficult at times for us to communicate through attorneys who are focused on protecting my rights as a citizen.

I want to be very clear on our family's position.

1.) We have no trust or confidence in the Boulder Police. They have tried, from the moment they walked in to our home on December 26, 1996, to convince others that Patsy or I or Burke killed JonBenét. I will hold them accountable forever for one thing—not accepting help from people who offered it in the beginning and who could have brought a wealth of experience to bear on this crime.

2.) We (myself, Patsy, Burke, John Andrew, Melinda) will meet anytime, anywhere, for as long as you want, with investigators from your office. If the purpose of a Grand Jury is to be able to talk to us, that is not necessary, We want to find the killer of our daughter and sister and will work with you twenty-four hours/day to find "it."

3.) If we are subpoenaed by a Grand Jury, we will testify, regardless of any previous meeting with your investigators.

I am living my life for two purposes, now: to find the killer of JonBenét and bring "it" to the maximum justice our society can impose. While there is a rage within me that says "Give me a few moments alone with this creature and there won't be a need for a trial," I would have succumbed to behavior which the killer did. Secondly, my living children must not have to live under the legacy that our "entertainment industry" has given them based on false information, and a frenzy centered on our family's misery to achieve substantial profit.

It's time to rise above all this pettiness and politics and get down to the most important mission—finding JonBenét's killer. That's all we care about. The police cannot do it. I hope it's not too late to investigate the case properly, at last.

Finally, I am willing and able to put up a

substantial reward ($1 million) through the help of friends if this would help drive information. I know this would be used against us by the media dimwits but if it would help, I don't care.

Please, let's do what is right to "get" this worst of all killers in our midst.

*Sincerely,
John Ramsey*

I had a telephone conversation with the district attorney on May thirtieth repeating that Patsy and I were available for more questioning at any time. To my amazement, a couple days later a story about our conversation appeared in the *Globe*. How did this information reach the tabloids?

Patsy and I agreed to additional extensive police interviews beginning June twenty-third, 1997, despite our attorney's strong objections. They simply did not trust the Boulder police and believed that to expose us to them anymore would be both fruitless and dangerous. The media gathered in hordes surrounding the Boulder Justice Center, and then the Broomfield Justice Center, where we were supposed to have met privately with the Boulder police. How did the media learn about our interviews and where they were to be held?

Our interviews lasted three days and were videotaped. It wasn't long before these tapes became public information on the Internet for anyone to watch. Who released them?

During the interrogations, Patsy and I were asked if we kept secrets from one another. The questions continued along that line until Patsy realized it was being implied that I had committed the murder and Patsy was covering for me, or vice versa. "You are going in the wrong direction!" she told them firmly. We were also each asked if we wondered, even for a moment, if the other could have murdered JonBenét. I answered in disgust "absolutely not for one second."

"If my husband ever harmed one of our children, I would have brought the curtain down on him long ago!" Patsy told them emphatically. The investigator hammered at Patsy, trying to break her down. He kept it up, but she stood up to him and held her own, refusing to be bullied. Her strong will was later publicly reported by the police with the conclusion that Patsy was someone who was capable of inner rage, and therefore murder. The so-called private interviews became public news with the lead headline that "police believe Patsy was capable of erupting in rage." There was no respite. It seemed like the entire world was against us, and nothing we did could stop the fury. To top it all off, at the University of Colorado, a former *Denver Post* newspaper editor lectured students describing JonBenét's murder as having "good entertainment value."

Summer began and Burke finished the 1997 school year, and we left Boulder forever. We left for our vacation home in Charlevoix hoping we could gather some peace and regain a sense of privacy. Of course, the media followed us and set up their cameras across the harbor in hotel rooms giving their telephoto lenses a clear view of our front porch.

The people of Charlevoix made us feel protected and safe; they gave us a sense of belonging and for Patsy and me, this was a sweet balm of healing. We felt secure and welcome, despite the media chaos we'd unwillingly brought with us that summer. This affection and loyalty were so sustaining that after Burke finished his sophomore year in an Atlanta area high school, we decided to make Charlevoix our year-round home. Burke was looking forward to attending Charlevoix High School and we looked forward to the wonderful quality of life this quiet lakeside community offered. Maybe Burke could actually get his childhood back now.

Not everything was dark and menacing in our lives. We had some heartening moments delivered by strangers such as the night we took Burke and his friends to a movie and out for burgers. By some miracle, we were able to dodge the media that night. In the restaurant, Patsy and I sat at one table and the boys at another. We both were feeling down that evening and we talked little, though the noise of the restaurant and the chatter of the boys were somewhat consoling. We tried to act normal for Burke's sake and were toying with our food when an elderly woman supported by a walker headed toward us. My heart stopped momentarily. I was very suspicious of any stranger entering our space. Was she going to verbally assault us in front of Burke and his friends? Patsy froze with her napkin at her mouth. "Oh, John, who is this headed our way?"

The woman came up to our table, pointed her finger at us, and said in a strident voice, "I know who you are. You two hang in there! Hang in there and don't give up!" And with a vigorous nod of the head, she turned with her walker and left the restaurant.

Immediately Patsy and I felt uplifted. Had this been a coincidence or an angel? We wanted to believe she was an angel, sent by God to encourage us just at the moment we really needed encouraging.

We experienced another similar encounter when we were walking down the street one early summer evening, headed for a dinner with friends. We were feeling very sad, and struggling to put on game faces before meeting our friends. I noticed a man crossing the busy street on a diagonal and aimed directly for us. Again my heart faltered. This had to be a reporter.

But the man had a kind, welcoming face. When he was within touching distance, he walked alongside us and said, "I just want to tell you that Jesus loves you." I started to say something besides thanks, but before I could, he turned, crossed the street, and vanished into the night. Was this another one of God's angels sent to encourage us?

Patsy and I felt as though the Lord Himself had reached down and given us each a kiss.

We cherished these two experiences and told ourselves perhaps God really hadn't forgotten us. We would never forget either face. Some people would call those touches just a coincidence. I think not.

So many things we should do. When would the police work to find the real killer of our child? How can I help? How many more interrogations must we go through? What was it I started to do? I can't remember. Be present, I tell myself. Focus only on today. There's the new day to get through.

Patsy makes pained breathy exclamations into her pillow as she sleeps. I know she's having a nightmare. I consider waking her, but reconsider. Which nightmare is worse, the living or the sleeping? Sleep should be an escape from the real nightmare we are dealing with. I hear the sound of bare feet on the wood floor, and our son, Burke, appears in the doorway, his disheveled hair caught in the streak of light cast through the drapes.

"Dad?"

"Hi, son."

"How come you're sleeping on the floor?" he asks, eyes wide, clear, innocent. He has his mother's emerald eyes.

Should I tell him I'd sleep on nails if I could? Should I tell him I can't bring myself to sleep in a soft bed so soon after JonBenét's death? I stroke his cheek. "Are you hungry, son?" What a question. It's five o'clock in the morning. "No," he murmurs, and nestles into my arms. Outside a ragged sky shreds through the edges of the drapes, and I can hear the moan of a morning dove.

We could stay here in our friends' house indefinitely, a proposition tempting, yet futile to ease our despair. I want to start with the small things.

Patsy, are we just dreaming this nightmare?

The real solution to our pain would be the sight of our little girl's face joining her brother's in the shadows of the doorway. So many Saturday mornings both of them jumping on our bed to wake us in anticipation of going out for breakfast, blueberry waffles and whipped cream. JonBenét with Jacques, the dog, trailing behind her. "Daddy! Daddy!"

I close my eyes now and I can hear her enthusiastic squeals, the happy sound of her voice. What will happen when I can no longer remember my child's voice? Wasn't life created with design? What of God's plan? Was it all a lucky or unlucky succession of culminated moments, a string of events taking in a random story to end right here? Did our lives end here? Would we ever look to the future with anticipation or would it always be with dread?

Burke lifts his face to mine, his large eyes, those emerald eyes of his mother, burning into mine, eyes that come alive when he laughs, then narrow suddenly as in thought, or fear. "Dad?"

"Mmm."

"Dad?" His gentle face, trembling mouth: "Will we be okay?"

I hold him and kiss the top of his head, looking for words, my son in my arms, both of us abstracted by a vision of the child who is missing.

Patsy will not get up with us. She cannot. She only recently stopped requiring other arms to help her to the bathroom. Sleep is still her only escape. Burke and I quietly make our way out of the room to the hallway, where an unshaded window reveals TV trucks, cars with reporters lurking in anticipation outside on the street. The sun, an absent stranger, cannot penetrate the gray sky, now a slab of slate. The world has never been this gray, this colorless, this turned in on itself. Burke and I pull into the shadows away from the prying cameras below.

A wind blows outside the window, and I watch the drooping boughs of the pine trees sway like women at a wake. A gust of old dead leaves brushes up against the line of hedges along the walk. Even the wind seems to be in a state of bereavement; each whiff against a branch of a tree rejects a dried leaf. I sit on the chair by the window, the shades now drawn to keep out reporters' eyes. Another day to face with pain yet to ease.

I drift into my memory and hear the voice of my daughter. "Daddy, why is the moon round?"

"Well, Johnnie Bee—"

"And how come the sun goes away at night?"

I hold my breath.

"Daddy?"

"Yes, honey."

"Daddy, where does it go?"

"Where does what go, honey?"

"The sun."

"It doesn't go anywhere, Sweetie—it—"

"Yes, it does! It goes to bed! The sun goes night-night! Mommy says so." And off she skips, chuckling happily, ponytail bobbing, to find her brother. I smile, watching her round the corner of the living room heading for the stairs. She always makes us laugh, this bright, funny child. Just last week she was explaining to us that smoke from candles is really prayers going up to Heaven. And last summer on our vacation in Mexico she taught us all how to do the Macarena.

"No, Daddy, that's not how you do it. Watch me!"

How she enjoyed my clumsiness. It was obvious to her I was no dancer.

Mommy caught on much quicker. Mommy wasn't self-conscious. Mommy and her little girl dancing, dressing up, singing, performing, having fun. They were beautiful together. Patsy, at five years old, had tap-danced in recitals and musicals, and she saw in JonBenét the same gusto for performing.

"If I ever have a daughter," she told her mother

when we were first married, "I'll teach her everything I know."

"What if she is nothing at all like you, Patsy?"

"Then I'll just have to teach her everything I *don't* know."

But JonBenét was just like Patsy in every way. Patsy wanted an original name for her daughter, so she chose my name, John, and my middle name, Bennett, put them together, and came up with JonBenét.

"I'm named after my daddy! Yay! I'm the only girl in kindergarten named after her daddy!"

Outgoing, full of energy, she took to performing like a bird to the air. Dressing up from the old antique trunk of dress-up clothes in the playroom, singing in costume with her cousins after dinner, playing different characters with her puppets. And the tomboy. Outside sliding down the hill with the boys. Sneakers and jeans, ponytail flying, her brother's little pal.

Patsy groans in her sleep on the bed and I'm awake. The wind outside the window has picked up. Its cold teeth can be felt in the darkening room. Shadows fall across the carpet like serrated knives.

Patsy turns fitfully in her sleep, then grabs my shoulder.

"John?"

"Yes, honey. I'm here."

"Did you lock the doors?"

"Yes. I locked the doors."

"The windows?"

"Yes, everything is locked tight."

"John?"

"Umm?"

"Who killed our baby?"

Fourteen years later I'd be jostling about in the back of an Indian-made TATA off-road vehicle along a potholed and rutted dirt road in Chitradurga, India, heading for the remote villages of poor Indian rice and sugarcane farmers. We come upon a snake crossing the road in front of us. Our Indian hosts scream, "Cobra, cobra!" We stop to watch the eight-foot snake slither across the road and then disappear into the dense teak forest. The cobra is one of the most venomous snakes in the world. In a single bite it can inject enough venom to kill an elephant, or up to twenty people. We watch in awe as the infamous snake slithers its way across the road, undulating in the sunlight, and finally disappearing into the teak forest. Patsy and I would have rather had this cobra to deal with than the media.

CHAPTER 6

Spiritual Roadblocks

Being a Christian is more than just an instantaneous conversion, it is a daily process whereby you grow to be more and more like Christ.
—Billy Graham

We make our way to church each week knowing reporters would be waiting at the door and sitting in the pews. One Jewish tabloid reporter went so far as to take communion kneeling next to us at the altar. We tried to find some humor in all the reporters and photographers that came to church with us, asking our minister if there was any kind of special award for bringing the most newcomers to church.

Why did I choose the Christian faith in the first

place? Originally, I thought I was born that way. I was born into a Christian family, so I just assumed I was a Christian. My mother took my brother, Jeff, and me to church when we were growing up, but we didn't get much out of it except to develop the impression that going to church is what you do when you get old. We made airplanes out of the offering envelopes, poked each other, played tic-tac-toe, and generally found it impossible to concentrate on the boring services. Attending church as kids did instill in us the idea that it is what good people don't mind doing, uncomfortable as it was.

The first six or seven years of my childhood were pretty normal for a kid growing up in Lincoln, Nebraska, where we had moved when my dad came home from World War II. It was a time when kids were safe to ride their bikes to Cunningham's Drugstore to get a marshmallow Coke at the soda fountain or buy cherry bomb firecrackers for the Fourth of July. The Cokes gave you cavities; the cherry bombs could blow off one of your fingers. But in those days, there weren't laws to protect us from ourselves, so if a child wanted to purchase what amounted to a small stick of dynamite, so be it. Ours was an ordinary, middle-class family, even though I thought we were better off than most people. Being rich, to my way of thinking, was simply a matter of having enough, plus a little extra.

Extra for me was the five cents my mother gave me to ride the city bus which stopped in front of our house, to the end of the line and back. It was my way of traveling the world, like my dad. Later I'd learn to fly an airplane like my dad; well, not exactly like him—he was the best pilot I've ever flown with.

My mother volunteered me as an acolyte in the church (to advance my spiritual growth). An acolyte is a boy or a girl who has certain ceremonial duties during an Episcopal church service. I wore a long red velvet robe (boiling in the Nebraska summers), and I carried in front of me, as reverently as I could, a highly polished mahogany pole about six feet long with a small flame on the end to light the church candles. With the sobriety of a monk, I proceeded down the aisle at the beginning of each service and lit six individual candles on separate stands with the long pole. There was always at least one candle that refused to light, and the pressure was on. I could feel every adult eye on me. The choir, the priest, and the cross bearer all waited impatiently in the narthex for me to complete my mission so they could parade triumphantly down the aisle with all candles successfully ablaze.

I was consigned to the tortures of an acolyte for an entire year. It taught me church is definitely not a fun place. During the service all I could think about was my next task. Circle around the altar, get the offering plates, wait for the offertory music after the solo, retrieve the offering plates, circle back, replace them. End of service, "Thanks be to God," get the candleholder, carry it back down the aisle, stand there until the priest and the assistant bow, then replace the candleholder on the wall, snap it safe, wait for music, oh, this was not fun, not fun at all. Being an acolyte was Spiritual Growth Roadblock Number One, the first of many spiritual growth roadblocks I would experience growing up.

Roadblock Number Two came when I was twelve. My best friend and I were in the midst of an intense box hockey game when he invited me to go to a youth fellowship meeting at his church that evening. Okay, sure, I said, but I was somewhat leery. After all, I thought the Episcopal Church was the only authentic church, and all other churches were the wrong ones and allegedly had very strange and bizarre rituals. I heard they did weird things like raise their hands, pray out loud right in church, and dunk people in tanks of water to baptize them. I went with a good deal of anxiety.

We arrived at the fellowship hall, and to my surprise, it was not scary at all. Cute girls, nice people. We played games, some older guy played the guitar, and I thought this could be okay until two men pulled me aside from the group and escorted me to a little side room and closed the door behind us.

I thought maybe I had done something wrong.

"You're new here, aren't you?"

"Yessir. What'd I do?"

"Are you Todd's friend?"

"Yessir." Maybe having Todd as a friend wasn't such a good idea, I thought. They asked my name, where I lived. I was scared. Maybe I could call my dad?

"Tell us, John. Are you saved?"

I didn't say anything. I had no idea what that meant. Saved? I needed to be saved from these guys, that was all I knew for absolute certain. I looked for ways to get out of the room.

The man repeated himself. "Are you saved, John?"

Struggling for the right answer, I blurted out, "Yes! I'm saved!" I waited. To my relief, I'd said the right thing. They smiled, pleased, patted me on the shoulder, said God bless you, and sent me back to the group in the fellowship hall.

I never went back to that church, and I can't remember if Todd and I remained friends. I was traumatized by the experience, and it would be years before I would learn what "saved" meant.

Once more my spiritual journey was impeded by well-meaning church people.

When I was in the eighth grade, our family moved to Okemos, Michigan, a small suburb of Lansing, when our dad was hired to run the Michigan Aeronautics Commission, a post he held until he retired. In the tenth grade, I started attending the high school youth fellowship at Okemos Community Church because my friends went there. I developed a crush on a girl two years older than me. I didn't dare ask her out on a date, of course. I barely had the nerve to talk to her. It came as heartbreak when I showed up at church one Sunday to find out that she and the minister had run off together the day before. It was a real scandal. Roadblock Number Three.

At Michigan State University, I was back in the pews of the Episcopal church in downtown Lansing because my new girlfriend was an Episcopalian and she insisted we go to church every Sunday. (I had forgotten all about the girl who ran off with the minister.) I was starting to believe that if I were truly a good person, I should be in church on Sundays with all the other truly good people. I willingly attended services, hardly missing a single Sunday. The priest, who stood at the door greeting the parishioners after the service, always would say to me, "Well, hello, young man! Is this the first time you've come to our church?" Every Sunday he asked me the same thing.

I feel that there are two places the question "Have you ever been here before?" should never be asked: a restaurant and a church. This was definitely bad for business. Even bars try to recognize a regular. Each time I went to church, I felt as if God didn't notice. That was Roadblock Number Four.

Eventually my girlfriend dumped me, and in my senior year, as president of Theta Chi fraternity, I had neglected church attendance entirely. I was focused on college life and graduation. But after our premier spring party, the Bowery Ball, two of my fraternity brothers and their dates were killed in a collision on the way home. This was my first experience with tragedy. My friends were young, talented, smart, full of promise, and now they were gone.

It was *unfair*.

We asked, *Why?* There's the famous question again, but none of us could come up with anything close to comforting. A couple of Campus Crusade for Christ counselors came to talk to us, and even though I was uncomfortable around religious people, these men seemed sincere, and they spent several hours talking with us, giving us assurances that helped, but didn't really answer the question

Why? As I listened to them, I began to ponder about life. *Does God have a purpose for our lives, and does He have a purpose for our deaths?* Do we live by chance, or are we here on earth until our life's purpose is fulfilled? I still went to church on Christmas and Easter. I prayed when I was in trouble. I gave a little bit to charities. I tried to be honest. I believed I was a good Christian, a good person. It began to occur to me that the many people I knew who were not Christian (my fraternity brothers who were atheists or Jewish, for example) were also honest, good people who gave to charities, and were kind, thoughtful human beings. I knew many non-Christian people who were exemplary people, loving, kind, and good—what made me, as a Christian, different?

The truth? At that point I *wasn't* different from anyone else. I was just another guy in the world navigating life as best I could. I went to church, yes, and maybe my atheist friends didn't go to church, but in the final analysis, we were quite a bit the same. We cared about the world, we cared about the environment, about our community; we were idealistic and desired to accomplish good things; the only difference between us was that I sat in church on Sundays and they didn't.

I graduated from college and married my college sweetheart, but in 1978, I was divorced from my college sweetheart and on my own with a dog, three children, and a station wagon. Where was the good life? My children, guided by my oldest daughter, Beth, looked after their dad, the one who had left the nest. Was I okay, was I doing all right? I loved my children dearly, and together we all struggled to find a sense of equilibrium. It was my first experience with loss.

After Patsy and I were married, I became more interested in things spiritual. I wanted more than the social aspect of church membership; I wanted the balm and cloak of the arms of the church over my life and family. Besides, at that point in my spiritual journey, I thought God would protect and bless me if I followed the rules and did those things a good Christian was supposed to do.

But now, here we were, in 1992, finally adjusted to our new lives, happy, and doing well, when Beth was killed. John Andrew and Melinda had to suffer not only the loss of their two-parent home, but also the loss of their sister. It was *unfair.*

We were all brokenhearted, and my cultural Christian faith proved empty and insignificant.

It took me four years after Beth's death to achieve some semblance of inner peace. I couldn't be alone or I would start to cry. Driving to and from work by myself, I would start to cry. Traveling on the airlines by myself, I would cry. The first year without her was the hardest. That first year facing her birthday, Christmas, Thanksgiving, the day of her death... almost too much for me. Beth's death caused me to examine my Christian faith intensely for the first time.

That is the part of my life story that only my close friends know. The part that much of the world knows is what occurred four years later. Four short years later.

CHAPTER 7

Faith Under Fire

*In this you greatly rejoice, though now for a little while,
if need be, you have been grieved by various trials, that the genuineness of your faith,* being *much more precious than gold
that perishes, though it is tested by fire, may be found to praise, honor, and glory at the revelation of Jesus Christ…*

—1 Peter 1:6-7

Job is the iconic biblical example of extreme suffering. He was successful, honest, faithful, and then he lost everything he had, including his ten children. His friends told him he must have done something that offended God to be punished so severely. His wife even turned against him and said, in desperate frustration, "Are you still holding on to your integrity? Curse God and die." Job replied, "Shall we accept the good from God, and not the trouble?" Job didn't have a single ally who believed in his innocence. Yet in his lonely despair, he remained faithful to God. This was an example of faith I was just beginning to recognize and understand.

God didn't cause Job's suffering. He allowed it but He wasn't punishing Job. This was an important thing for me to understand. *God does not cause our suffering.*

Most of our suffering generates from the unfairness in life. I don't know at what age we start to notice that life seems to have it in for us. Kids tease us at school, we fall down and hurt ourselves, we get sick, our teacher doesn't like us, our skin breaks out just when we start to get interested in the opposite sex, we get picked last when teams are being chosen. The unfairness! We begin to wonder about ourselves; we wonder, whether consciously or unconsciously, what's wrong with me?

But there's nothing wrong with us. Life simply isn't always fair. God put us on the earth to deal with the unfairness of life armed with His strength, power, and wisdom, but forewarns us that life will be difficult at times. Job asked God *Why?* but he did not get an answer.

Patsy and I asked *Why? Why* was our child murdered? *Why* did the police accuse us? Why did the Boulder police not investigate all the leads that came to them? *Why?*

The police began leaking biased and false information to the media, always as an "unnamed source, close to the investigation." A rookie detective with only six months on the job gave a confidential interview to *Vanity Fair* magazine within weeks of JonBenét's death and clearly implicated us as the killers.

The actual evidence conflicted with the impetuous conclusion of the police, and that became a problem for them. There was *foreign male* DNA. The footprints and handprints did not match anyone in our family, plus the open window and door were evidence enough that an intruder had entered our home that night. The butler pantry door was open, and the killer may have escaped through that door. There was not one bit of *evidence* to cast a shadow of suspicion on us—it had all been supposition.

Statistically in the United States, in the case of serious child injury or murder, 68 percent of the time a caregiver is responsible. Within that 68 percent segment, in virtually all of those cases, there is a long history of abuse leading up to the death of the child. The schools are usually suspicious of abuse; the police are aware of abuse because they have more than likely been called to the home on occasion. The family doctor is required to report any signs of child abuse. The neighbors are usually aware of abuse and neglect. It's really no secret when there's trouble in a home. But if there has been no history of physical or verbal abuse, no alcohol or drug abuse, no parental discord, no odd behavior of the children, no discord in the home, the chances of a parent committing such a horrible crime are extremely rare.

We were a happy, peaceful, loving family celebrating Christmas.

They didn't see that.

The story of Job addresses issues that we all have to deal with when tragedy strikes. Do we still trust and have faith in God when we are being battered by life? When we have done nothing to deserve the trials we are faced with? Can we be satisfied without getting an answer to the question *Why?* For me, the most astounding detail in the Book of Job comes at the end of the story. Because of Job's faithfulness despite hardship, God restores everything Job had *twofold.* God gave Job twice as many cattle, sheep, and goats as he had before. The story ends with God giving Job ten children, exactly the number he had in the beginning. Wait, why not twenty, which would be twofold, just as with everything else? If Job asked God why He didn't give him twenty children, God would have told him, "My son, you do have twenty children, ten are with you on earth, and ten are with me in Heaven." It is consistent with the message Jesus brought us twenty-five hundred years later about eternal life. This detail staggered me with how amazing God is. It gave me comfort that, like Job, two of my children are with God in Heaven, and three are here with me on earth.

It was Christmas 1991 in Atlanta, and an especially enjoyable time for our family. We were celebrating my daughter Melinda's debutante coming-out event, an old Southern tradition of introducing a young woman to society. It was a wonderful father-daughter season. Melinda and I attended lunches and small parties with the other girls and their fathers. For the culminating event, there was a formal dinner dance. Beth brought her special friend, Matt, for us to meet for the first time.

Melinda was thrilled to have her sister take part in her special event, and I can still see the girls in their ball gowns whispering and giggling together on the ballroom floor. (Patsy's mind was already working on how to create a fabulous wedding for Beth.)

The next day, Beth and Matt said good-bye to us with kisses and hugs. Ten days later, January 8, 1992, they traveled to Matt's family home in Chicago so Beth could meet his parents. They were driving along on a slippery on-ramp about to enter the freeway—

My brother called me at the office to tell me about the accident, and the first words I screamed were, "There is no God! There is no God!" How could a loving God let this happen?

I was furious with God. My immature faith in God plummeted to bedrock. God should have been paying attention when that truck loomed before their car, before the crash, the ripping of metal, the shattering of glass, the screaming tires—

And now here it was, years later, when I'd see that I've lived under the false notion that the really bad things in life happened to *other* good people. My question was not why do bad things happen to good people, but why did bad things happen to *this* good person? At night when we turned on CNN before bed, the personal tragedies we watched didn't affect me at all. We could turn off the ten o'clock news after hearing about a family's life thrown into a tailspin when a son was killed by a drunk driver, and still manage to sleep soundly, and the next day forget the story entirely. Much the same as other viewers while sitting in their easy chairs or lying in their warm beds would watch how a precious little six-year-old girl had been murdered on Christmas Day. Now I was on the inside of the television screen.

One day I was sublimely content with my successful business, a married cocoon of bliss, not particularly mindful of the woes of the world, and the next day the cocoon burst apart and grief overtook my universe.

I had to fill my mind with something besides grief. A seventeen-year-old boy shared this poem he wrote to honor his stillborn baby sister, and it helped.

Through heaven's gate you dance with mirth, and through
    a glowing hall,
    on such splendor as is not on earth, you gazed upon in awe.
    There you heard the Angels harps, there the Saints did sing,

there above all sparkling stars, you knelt before the King.
There the gladsome laughter rang, rejoicing round the throne,
loud songs of praise the Cherubs sang,
for a child of God come home.
Although we're left to weep a day and mourn in this world of men,
Heaven rings with your shouts of play, and we shall meet again.

—Travis Vick (used by permission)

Yes, we will meet again. That is a promise I accept as absolute truth.

My mind would wander. Beth, singing and practicing cartwheels in the backyard to the music of the Beach Boys on her cassette recorder. JonBenét trying to keep up with Burke and his friends in backyard games.

Had I memorized their faces well enough? Could I recount Beth's smile? Could I lie here now on the floor and bring forth the sound of her voice: *"Hi, Dad—I love you, Dad—you're the best dad in the whole world—hugs, Dad..."* How much of our children's lives do we forget? How much do we keep close to us? Could I recount to you now even a hundredth of the countless joyous moments with my children?

JonBenét at four years old:

"What did you do today, Johnnie Bee?"

"Me and Mommy learned a new song!"

"Mommy and I."

"Okay, but first let me sing you me and mommy's song."

Beth at ten years old:

"So, honey, how was school today?"

"Okay."

"Just okay?"

"Tiffany isn't my best friend anymore, and I hate math."

JonBenét at five years old:

"What did you do at preschool today, sweetheart?"

"We colored."

"Oh? And what did you color?"

"A bird and a tree and hearts."

Beth at fifteen years old:

"How are you doing in your classes, dear?"

"Oh, Dad, I met the cutest guy! I think he likes me, and oh yeah, I made the cheerleading squad."

JonBenét at six years old:

"So, Johnnie Bee, how's my kindergartner?"

"Daddy! Oh, Daddy, I just love school. First of

all, I'm the only girl in the entire school named after her daddy and it's so much fun, and we get to sing songs and do art and—"

Beth at seventeen years old:

"Hi, honey. How's my girl?"

"Dad, I was elected captain of the cheerleading squad, and I've gained two and one-eighth pounds."

Years clumped together with only remnants of diaries, photographs, rings, school yearbooks, ribbons, a child's rocker, a tiny ballet slipper to remind me that my girls were now among the dead. My sweet daughters I thought would live forever.

Most people go through life expecting it to extend indefinitely. Why else do we set up a college savings plan for our children, or help them in every way possible to succeed in life, if it's not that we believe in their future? The future is very much a daily reality. I don't know about you, but I've lived much of my life more in the future than the present, always working toward something more, something better, something higher, loftier.

Had Beth's twenty-two years and JonBenét's short six years on earth fulfilled God's purpose for them? My infant faith was in a nosedive after Beth's death, and I wondered if I ever really believed in God. I walked the floor of our living room, stared up at the ceiling fan, the pictures on the wall—if there was really a God, who was He? Does He allow evil and death and tragedy to punish us? Dostoyevsky observed that "the death of a single infant calls into question the existence of God," and Dostoyevsky was supposed to have been a Christian believer, same as me. Or was I really a believer?

I can't imagine any human pain worse than losing a child. It isn't natural that parents bury their child. It is simply not the way it's supposed to be! A parent never really goes back to normal after the death of a child. One young mother, whose six-year-old son had been killed while riding his bike near home, told me, "It's like I have a hole in my heart that won't heal." I understood, of course. It's called a broken heart.

A broken heart.

We were faced with living with broken hearts because of loss we could not have imagined. Didn't God know that no child should precede a parent in death?

I asked all of the questions that I know the Lord of the Universe is accustomed to hearing. I assailed Him with *Why did you let this happen? Aren't you supposed to protect us? Where were you? Why? Why? Why?* (That question, *Why?*)

I wore myself out asking questions when Beth died. I exhausted myself crying; I was emptied and sickened with asking, with begging, with crying. I just wanted my daughter back. Never mind why, just bring her back. Give me back my daughter.

What I needed was to really understand God and what He promised, and what He didn't promise.

But the biggest challenge was still ahead.

CHAPTER 8

God and Healing

*O LORD my God, I cried out to You,
And You healed me.*
—Psalm 30:2

Two years after the loss of Beth, I was beginning to recover—well, not exactly recover, but at least living with its reality, when Patsy was diagnosed with ovarian cancer. It was 1994.

Patsy had been going to a chiropractor for shoulder pain, and when her stomach began to swell, she sought help from her Boulder gynecologist, but she was unable to identify the disease. We went to Atlanta to visit Patsy's parents, and her mother took one look at her and said, "There is something very wrong here and we are going to find out what it is." They immediately left for the emergency room at Northside Hospital, and within thirty minutes the doctor discovered a large baseball-sized tumor in her lower abdomen. The next day it was confirmed to be malignant.

We were shocked by the news. Patsy was only thirty-eight years old. She worried more about how I would handle the news than about herself. She told her doctor, "John doesn't need this. He's still reeling from his daughter's death."

Cancer, accidents—these things should not happen to good people. How could cancer happen to such a good person as Patsy?

Had the stress and pain of the loss of Beth brought this on? There is a school of thought that relates stress to a reduced immune system, which leads to the opportunity for abnormal cancer cells to begin to develop.

The onset of Patsy's cancer came to us as a bolt from the blue along with a blizzard of unrelenting questions beginning with the prince of questions, *Why?* JonBenét was only four years old. Burke was seven. "John, will I see my children graduate high school? Will I be here for JonBenét's wedding? Will I be dead before they're teenagers?" Her face pressed hard against my chest as she wept.

"My babies will be motherless! I'll never be a grandmother! Why would God give me these two beautiful children to take me away from them and leave them motherless?"

There was no comforting her. She didn't want to leave her children and she would fight with all her might to stay. "For their sake, please, God, don't take me. And don't take me from my husband. He needs me. Oh God."

"Patsy, we'll get through this. We'll get through this." But I was scared. We were both scared.

That night before going to sleep, Patsy read out loud from the Bible, Psalm 38:

Do not forsake me, O LORD;
 O my God, be not far from me!
 Make haste to help me,
 O Lord, my salvation!

Yes, Lord, don't forsake us. Heal Patsy. Let her live, Lord. We need her. JonBenét needs her. Burke needs her. John Andrew needs her. Melinda needs her. And, oh Jesus, I need her.

I thought the world needed Patsy, too, such a kind, dear person. Patsy was the most trusting, open-hearted, thoughtful person I had ever known. People loved her because she was genuinely caring and good. She often described herself as "what you see is what you get." She opened our home to everyone the way she opened her heart, and here was where we later asked ourselves if she hadn't opened a bit too much. Had she opened our home to a murderer? Had she unwittingly made it easy for a killer to know the rooms of our home?

Do not forsake me, O LORD...

Since facing the daunting questions I'd asked after Beth died—Who was God? Is there a God? What did He promise us?—I had started to grow spiritually. I didn't have a lightning bolt moment as some people do. My spiritual journey was slow and gradual. One day, I just crossed that line between doubt and faith, and now my young faith was being tested again. I was supposed to be the strong one. I was the husband, the man of the house. I had no words, no answers. In my arms, I held the sweet love of my life, who was facing the possibility of death. I had no words.

I did everything I could to find the best treatment for Patsy. I researched every opportunity, every program of every treatment center I could find. One day she was here getting ready to go see the Fourth of July fireworks, and the next day she was in the hospital having a radical hysterectomy to see how bad the cancer was.

It was bad. It was Stage Three.

I held Patsy's hand as tears rolled down her face. She tried to smile. "Well, honey, we can be thankful it isn't Stage Four, right?"

"Yes, darling. It's only Stage Three."

I tried to think clearly. Surely there was something I could do. A surgeon friend of ours told us about a treatment his mother-in-law had successfully undergone. It was a radical experimental treatment at the National Cancer Institute.

Two weeks later I took Patsy to the National Cancer Institute in Bethesda, Maryland, hoping we could get her enrolled in the treatment program. She was again examined and a tumor the size of a golf ball was discovered lodged behind her pelvic bone, and the cancer had spread to her lymph nodes. You don't want to hear Stage Four. Stage One, Two, or Three, but not Stage Four. People don't live long with Stage Four.

Patsy had Stage Four ovarian cancer. I was informed that, statistically, Patsy had only a 5 percent chance to survive more than a few years.

We wanted to begin the treatment programs immediately. Cancer sufferers don't want to wait. They need to start attacking the disease immediately—to wait just gives the cancerous cells more time to grow. High doses of Taxol, Cysplatin, and Cytoxin were to be administered monthly for the better part of a year. Each chemotherapy session lasted thirty-six hours because the chemicals could not be injected any faster or they possibly would kill her. As harrowing as it was, we were grateful for this program and clung to the hope for a miracle.

We had one day before the chemotherapy program began, so I took her to a small historic bed-and-breakfast in Annapolis for that night, hoping to give our minds a diversion and make a plan. There I was again, the businessman, thinking all we needed was a plan, a strategic proven chart of action to follow perfectly, and she'd get well. All I needed to do was to figure out our plan of attack against this enemy in her body.

That evening after a dinner we barely touched, Patsy stretched out on the bed in our room and reached for the Gideon Bible in the nightstand drawer. She read for a while as I hovered over my laptop researching cancer treatment details.

"John, listen to this: *'In the shadow of Your wings I will make my refuge, Until these calamities have passed by.'*"

"What was that? Read it again."

"*'In the shadow of Your wings I will make my refuge—'* John, that's it! He's our only hope. The doctors can only do so much."

I sat up, stared at her. "I'm sorry, sweetheart. What are you saying? Is that one of those Gideon Bibles you're reading?"

"Yes! I think God is speaking to us here. This is God's word! John, I need to take refuge in Him!

'Until these calamities have passed by'!"

Her words hit me like rain. "Refuge in God—yes!"

"This verse, John, talks about calamities *passing by*. I mean, like they won't last, they'll *pass by*. Oh, I'm sure this verse is the Lord speaking to us, encouraging us. I never saw this verse before. It's Psalm 57:1. I just need to trust Him!"

We held each other, shed a few more tears, and I prayed. "Lord, I place my wife in Your arms to help and to heal. Be her refuge, Lord, and we will trust You until these calamities have passed by."

"Amen," Patsy whispered, and then she smiled, gave me a kiss, and said, "Hey, this is a nice place you've brought me to. I didn't notice a thing around me until now. What'd we have for dinner?"

"I don't remember."

"Ha! Call room service."

We slept soundly that night, and we knew it was due to the presence of God in the room, and the faith that the Holy Sprit had planted in us with that one single Bible verse. It was a truth that even as I held my sleeping wife in my arms, God would be the one to hold her and lift her up through this ordeal, not me. I had no power against this disease, none. No doubt about it, God was calling me to have more faith. If I was going to help Patsy through this ordeal, I had better step up my relationship with God.

Patsy began her first chemotherapy treatment on July 27, 1994, and it lasted thirty-six hours. After her first chemotherapy treatment in Bethesda, two-and-a-half years before we were to lose JonBenét, Father Rol, the priest from our church, called and asked if he and some friends might come over and have a healing service for Patsy. They came through the front door with their Bibles and confident faces, and I welcomed them eagerly. Patsy, weak as mist, lay upstairs under the covers in our third-floor bedroom. Father Rol stood in our vestibule, and said, "I believe God can heal Patsy. That's why we want to have a healing service for her."

"Yes, a healing service," I agreed.

"Do you believe God can heal Patsy?"

"Of course. I've been praying—"

"So have many of us in the church. So let's get at it!"

We climbed up the stairs to our room. The people gathered around Patsy, who managed to make it to a straight-back chair breathing with difficulty and trying to smile. They laid hands on her, and Father Rol read from Isaiah 53 in the Bible.

Surely He has borne our griefs
  And carried our sorrows;

*Yet we esteemed Him stricken,
Smitten by God, and afflicted.
But He* was *wounded for our transgressions,
He* was *bruised for our iniquities;
The chastisement for our peace* was *upon Him,
And by His stripes we are healed.*

Are healed. That's present tense. Of course I knew Jesus died for me and that if I believed in Him I'd have eternal life, but I'd never heard about *healing.*

As the people prayed, I felt a peace and sincerity enter the room, like a soothing brush of a palm across the forehead.

What was happening? On they prayed:

"Father God, we are standing on Your word that tells us by the stripes of Jesus, Patsy is healed..."

"In the name of Jesus."

Patsy raised her arms. She began praying out loud, "Lord, I receive Your healing. I receive the healing of my body. I thank you, Lord."

The people prayed on, as Father Rol's gentle voice filled the room, his heartfelt way of praying to Jesus so intimate and personal. I felt as if we were standing on holy ground. Patsy was submerged in prayer. I prayed as fervently and devoutly as I could. I wanted Patsy to be healed more than anything, but I wasn't sure if God would hear our prayers.

Back in Bethesda two days later, Patsy had a CT scan, and to the doctors' amazement, the golf ball–sized tumor was completely gone. Vanished. Erased. Not there! Patsy exclaimed to the doctors that God had healed her. There was no visible trace of cancer. Patsy told her doctors she no longer needed the chemo treatments! The doctors were encouraged and amazed, but insisted she'd have to endure six more treatments of the demanding chemo treatments and more CT scans just to be sure.

So every three weeks she flew from Denver to Bethesda for three days of chemotherapy, which was administered through a porta-cath tube surgically implanted in her chest. After the treatment, she flew back home to Boulder, so nauseous she could barely sit up. It was a three-and-one-half-hour flight, and somehow miraculously, there was always an empty row of seats so she could lay her head down until the plane landed. We were grateful for anything that would ease her excruciating discomfort. When I couldn't accompany her on these exhausting trips due to my work, her mother would travel with her and try to keep her spirits up. At home we all had to wear surgical masks when she returned because most of her white blood cells had been killed by the chemotherapy. Even a minor infection could be deathly serious.

When each of Patsy's thirty-six-hour treatments finished, her white blood cells would be so low she would have to be admitted to the Boulder Community Hospital for a week for bone marrow stimulants, and blood transfusions. By the third week of treatment she would be well enough to come home for a few days before going back to Bethesda. She used to joke that the doctors at the National Cancer Institute would inject enough chemotherapy poison to nearly kill her and then it was her oncologist in Boulder who had to fight to keep her alive.

I took the kids to visit her in the hospital and it was so traumatic for her to see them leave her that I felt like crying with her. "Mommy's getting all better," I tried to assure them. "That's why she's in the hospital." JonBenét wanted to know if Jesus was a doctor. The question surprised me and I couldn't help smiling. "Well, yes, honey, yes, in a way. I mean, He's our invisible doctor—um, how about we go bring Mommy some pizza?"

She asked the same question of Patsy. "Mommy, is Jesus a doctor?"

Without hesitating, Patsy responded, "He's the best doctor, sweetheart. He's going to heal Mommy."

"I thought the hospital was going to heal you."

"Jesus is right here in the hospital. In fact, He's everywhere. Jesus will heal me in the hospital or wherever I am."

Burke liked that answer, too, and the four of us ate our pizza in the family waiting room. (I think I actually saw Patsy take a bite or two.) She had lost all her hair by now and wore a little turban, and JonBenét decided she wanted one just like it.

Six treatments later, still no sign of disease.

But that wasn't the end of it. When Patsy had completed her treatment regimen, she came home for Christmas and then the following day returned to Bethesda for a laparotomy, which is a surgery that opens the body from the breastbone to the pelvis to extract tissue samples and do a cavity wash in order to be absolutely positive there are no malignant cells hidden anywhere else in the body. She had her thirty-ninth birthday and New Year's Eve in the ICU in excruciating pain, and on morphine.

Two more chemotherapy treatments "just for good measure," the doctors said, and she was home clear. My poor girl. I kept thinking if the cancer didn't kill her, those terrible treatments would. But we both knew that it wasn't the treatments alone that healed her, but God Himself. Even her oncologist wrote to us years later that he, too, believed that Patsy had been healed by God.

There was no question in his mind. He had seen how bad the cancer was when he opened her up the first time. My beloved, brave girl was home clear. She was completely cancer free. I was beginning to see God at work in our lives. It had to be God.

The calamity that Psalm 57 talked about had indeed passed, just as it had said it would. The previous summer in the Annapolis hotel room, God had spoken to us through those words and we had clung to them. *Thank you, Lord, thank you.*

You're welcome, my son, you're welcome.

CHAPTER 9

Love, Divorce, and Grace

The LORD is good,
a stronghold in the day of trouble;
And He knows those who trust in Him.
—Nahum 1:7

When Gerald R. Ford took the oath of office as President of the United States on August 9, 1974, he declared, "I assume the presidency under extraordinary circumstances…" The personal circumstances in my life at the time were in the form of a struggling new business, and by the time Jimmy Carter came into office fours years later, my first marriage was failing. "This is an hour of history that troubles our minds and hurts our hearts," President Ford exclaimed, and Jimmy Carter, who succeeded him, took office combating the continuing economic woes of inflation, unemployment, and 20 percent interest rates. As he was handling the Camp David agreement of 1978 to bring amity between Egypt and Israel, my college sweetheart and I were signing divorce papers. Don't let anyone understate it, divorce is horrible. I was devastated and worried I wouldn't be able to be near my three children as they grew up. I felt like a total failure, both as a husband and as a father. The world situation disheartened us with the reports of U.S. embassy staff seized as hostages in Iran, and while history troubled our minds and hearts, I had to figure out how to navigate a new life separated from my three children.

I grew a beard and bought a Porsche.

My former father-in-law died early that year, which distressed the entire family, and if that wasn't enough, a few months later my sweet mother died at the age of fifty-nine of complications related to colon cancer.

My Porsche was no comfort.

Divorced, and with nowhere else to go, I moved in with a friend and slept on the floor in his small apartment. You think you want something different, you think the grass is greener elsewhere, but that supposed "greener grass" is fantasy. Then you find yourself sleeping on someone's floor with your Porsche out front, no children in the house, and you're sure, at thirty-four years old, you're the biggest failure to ever walk the earth.

I remember sitting in the crowded airport on my way back to Atlanta after my mother's funeral trying to keep from crying. I hadn't realized how much I depended on the faithful love and support of my mother. She had instilled in me a solid confidence that I had something important to contribute to the world because she believed I was a good son, a good man, and I made her proud. The thought of not seeing her again, not hearing her voice again, crushed my spirit. Sitting there, I realized it was imperative that I make a contribution to the world that was worthy of the sacrifices my mother made for me during my childhood.

I told my roommate I hoped that neither he nor anyone else would have to face such a lousy year: Divorce, two deaths, kids living apart, how much could one guy take? I would never have dreamed by any stretch of my imagination the horror that lay ahead for me. I thought this was as bad as it gets. If I recovered from this, I thought, I could handle anything.

I visited our family's summer cabin on Lake Mecosta, Michigan, the next spring, and at night I stood at the end of our old dock staring into the clear night sky asking God for a sign that there was a Heaven and that my mother was there. I asked Him to send a shooting star as my answer. I wanted to know for sure my mother was happy somewhere, that she wasn't simply gone forever and ever, and that there was more to life than just this earthly life. I needed to know if there really was a Heaven and a God, and I guess I was asking God to prove it to me.

After standing at the end of the dock for a long time, I turned to go back to the cabin, and there, shooting across the cobalt sky, came a faint shooting star. Yes, it was real. A shooting star.

God speaks to us in different ways, and He spoke a blessing loud and clear into my life in the spring of 1979 when I met Patsy. She was from the small town of Parkersburg, West Virginia, had graduated from West Virginia University with a major in journalism, and had moved to Atlanta to start a career in the advertising business. I had no idea when we met that she has been Miss West Virginia and was a participant in the 1977 Miss America Pageant in Atlantic City. Patsy was twenty-two years old with a full life ahead of her, and I was a divorced thirty-five-year-old man with three children, a dog, and a Porsche. To my delight, she liked me, and from our first date I knew she was unlike any girl I had ever met. She had an internal beauty that radiated. Her small-town graciousness, vivacious personality, sense of humor, and *joie de vivre* were genuine, and when a friend told me Patsy had won one of the top ten talent awards in the Miss America Pageant, I was surprised. She was positively effervescent, but when I looked for pride or conceit, I found none.

Her talent that year in Atlantic City was oratory. "No one ever wins with a dramatic reading," she said, laughing when I asked her about it. "You have to be able to sing, and that left me out," she said with a shrug and a sigh. "I was a small-town girl, just thrilled to be there, but I did manage to win scholarship money for my college tuition."

She smoothed a hair behind her ear. "However, if someday in the far future I have a daughter, and she wants to follow the beauty pageant path, fine," she said with prophetic naïveté. "I'll do all I can to help her because it's really a positive and wonderful experience."

Neither one of us could have imagined the ominous foreshadowing in her words.

"And as for me?" she said, laughing. "I always say it's better to be a has-been than a never-was."

I became the enamored love-struck, goofy guy dating Patsy. She was a true lady, charming, and a delight to be around, but I discovered there was more to her than just her charm and her grace. There was an honesty and considerate quality to her personality that drew me. I remember our dating days with fondness as I try to relive the happiness this fine twenty-two-year-old girl created around herself.

We dated for a year, and on the day I asked her to marry me, I rehearsed my proposal and had everything planned perfectly. I had already spoken to her father to ask his permission, to impress him with my good intentions and follow good old Southern customs. I borrowed money from my dad to buy an engagement ring and made a dinner reservation at a romantic candlelit restaurant framed by a golden tulip poplar tree in the suburb of Vinings, Georgia. Soft music, an expensive menu, a table by the window, it was perfect. This was the ideal prelude to a proposal.

We ordered our meal and I sat grinning and trying to make small talk like an idiot. I think she thought I was sick. I could barely touch my food. After dabbing our chins with our napkins, I took her arm and we walked outside and sat in a rustic little gazebo with white paint flaking off the seat, the stars sparkling overhead through the branches of the tree, and the slight smell of tulip nectar filling the night air. I was nervous and probably sweating a little, but just like in the movies, with ring in hand I went right to the point. "Patsy, will you marry me?"

I waited for her answer, expectantly. Surely she'd leap into my arms (like in the movies) and tell me how her dreams had finally come true. "Yes, yes!" she would exclaim.

That's not what happened. She nodded, sighed, and said, "I'll have to talk to my mother first."

Talk to her mother! Had I heard right? *Deflated* is the word that comes to mind. Days went by, and my male ego was eroding by the minute. What was I thinking? Here I was, a divorced man with three children, and I was thirteen years older than Patsy. Would Patsy's family want a man like me in their pure, innocent daughter's life?

When I finally received Patsy's answer of yes, I became the happiest man in Atlanta. Her family said they were pleased with Patsy's choice of a husband, and gave us their love and blessing.

I called the Episcopal cathedral I had attended occasionally for an appointment to come and discuss our wedding. The priest's voice on the telephone was a little frosty. I had hoped he'd be happy for me. "You'll have to come in for an interview before we can proceed," he said.

I walked up the shrub-lined sidewalk to the church office and took a seat in the reception area, a room of stiff-backed chairs and a large plastic plant in the corner by the window. I felt uncomfortable, as though something wasn't right. I wanted to be married in the Episcopal Church with God's blessing, and I felt joy and expectancy I'd never felt in my life. This was a significant step in restarting my life after the train wreck of my divorce. Surely God had smiled on me and was giving me a second chance at love and life.

The priest, after a few minutes of introductory chitchat, questioned me about my divorce.

"Divorce?" I explained the whole thing as best I could. He listened without smiling or comment.

"Because you are a divorced man, I will have to get the bishop's permission before we can proceed with a marriage. I don't know if he will approve."

I left his office of dark wood and musty carpeting feeling like I must be a very bad person. I wasn't good enough to be married in such a holy place. I left wishing I had asked more questions. I told him the divorce was a failure on my part, but hadn't God forgiven me? Hadn't God blessed me with a new life? I thought churches were a place for good people, and I was trying to be one of them. The priest, with his arms folded across his black-shirted chest, staring at me through judging eyes, said, in effect, "Sorry, you are not good enough to be married in our church. We're too holy for you."

I sat in my car staring at the steering wheel. How ironic, I thought, as I looked out at the bending willow trees and the expanse of green grass surrounding this church of God. In the sixteenth century, the Episcopal Church was started by England's King Henry VIII in order to get a church-approved divorce from Catherine of Aragon so he could marry Anne Boleyn. The Catholic Church, the official Church of England at the time, had steadfastly refused to approve King Henry's divorce. King Henry simply disenfranchised the Catholic Church as the official Church of England and formed his own church as the new official Church of England and got his divorce approved by the new church. One of the positive outcomes of this move was the introduction of the English-language Bible, which had been translated by William Tyndale but previously banned by the Catholic Church in England. In time, this new Church of England became the Episcopal Church in other parts of the world. I drove back to my apartment wondering if the good priest had forgotten his church history.

Please understand I'm not criticizing the Episcopal Church, because I've always loved the church and its history and rituals. You never forget your roots. There are tenets and by-laws and rules of every denomination, and I accept that.

My next call was to the Peachtree Presbyterian Church, which at the time was one of the largest Presbyterian churches in the United States. Reverend Dr. Frank Harrington, the senior minister, took my call and opened his arms in love to Patsy and me and told us he would be honored to marry us. We had a beautiful wedding, and promptly became members of his church. In Reverend Harrington, I saw that God is loving and good, that He is kind, forgiving, and not judgmental. We felt welcome and accepted and became active in the adult Sunday school class. The friends we made in that class are friends to this day.

We attended Sunday school classes, but I was so ignorant about the Bible that when the teacher said something like "Now turn in your Bibles to the book of Ecclesiastes," I had no idea where that was. Old or New Testament? I'd watch out of the corner of my eye to see what part of the Bible everyone else was turning to, and then I'd figure out which direction to look, front or back.

One day after church Patsy, who was about twenty-four at the time, stood with her arms around my three children. A woman said to her, "You look amazing for a woman with three children! Are they yours?"

"Yes!" Patsy responded. "They're mine."

Patsy loved my children as if they were her own,

and they loved her back. A few years later I became an elder at Peachtree Church, and our lives grew quite settled and content. I had a growing business, and we were actually able to put a little money in the bank. We were married for seven years before our son, Burke, was born. Seven romantic, happy, busy years, and the crowning glory of our years together was when we knew we were going to have a child. If it was a boy, Patsy wanted to name him Hamilton. I didn't object, but one night during her pregnancy I had a dream. In the dream I saw a book before me, a huge book. The pages of the book were open and I heard a voice, a man's voice. "The name shall be Burke," said the voice.

I awoke astonished by the dream. I had never heard the name *Burke*. I had never had a dream like that. Whom did we know named Burke? That's a boy's name, right? And who was that who'd spoken to me? How did he know we were having a son? What if it was a girl? The dream puzzled me, but Patsy recognized it immediately as a direct message from Heaven.

"You think it was God, Patsy?"

"I do. And so it's settled. His name will be Burke."

I nodded. "Burke Hamilton."

True to the dream, Patsy gave birth to a son, and Burke Hamilton was born January 27, 1987.

Three years later, Patsy gave birth to JonBenét, who quickly became the spark plug in our family. We marveled at how much she took after her mother. Burke was like his dad, more reserved and quiet. Now, our children added up to five. Our life was good, better than good. I was making money and I had a beautiful family; could it get any better than this?

I concentrated on building up the material foundation for our lives, and relegated the spiritual part for later. We went to church and that made us Christians, so I figured we were in good stead in that department. I was building a business, looking forward to getting a bigger house; I was increasing my bank account; I was providing for my growing family. This was an important time of life for a man. If you don't build now, when will you? I was responsible. I sold the Porsche.

What could happen that a good job and money couldn't handle?

CHAPTER 10

Regrets

He sent from above, He took me;
He drew me out of many waters.
He delivered me from my strong enemy.
—Psalm 18:16–17

I started my computer business in 1982 in the basement of our home in Atlanta. Patsy worked with me as secretary, office manager, sales manager, and any other title I could give her. We were a true mom-and-pop organization. One day a potential customer arrived, thinking she was going to a real office in a real office building, and was quickly disappointed when she was directed around the back of our house to the basement door, and found us there hard at work in our makeshift office. We got a good laugh when she took one look at our setup and scurried back across the yard to her car. With our golden retriever galloping behind her, it was quite a sight.

We worked hard drumming up sales for our products, and the business grew. Eventually our Atlanta neighbors complained about the tractor-trailer trucks pulling up in front of our house with shipments, the zoning inspector showed up, and we had to move to a real office. We eventually merged with two other companies and became Access Graphics. That merger eventually required that we move to Boulder, Colorado.

I always worried about money. Even after the company hit twenty million dollars in sales per month, I worried. What if? What if the company failed? What if? That was 1991.

I had been commuting back and forth from Atlanta to Boulder for a year before we decided to make our permanent home in Boulder. We weren't happy about leaving Atlanta, where we'd lived for so many years, but since I was now president of the newly merged company, we thought it was the best choice for our little family. With our two young children, ages one and four, we packed up, sold our Atlanta home, and headed to the small university town at the foot of the Rocky Mountains thinking the best was yet to come.

And it was the best.

For a while.

My children from my first marriage, Beth, John Andrew, and Melinda, would visit often, and we'd have a great time hiking, bicycling, skiing, and enjoying our new Colorado outdoor life. Patsy adored my older children and so did JonBenét and Burke, and they were always sad when they left to go back to their homes. The unhappy days were over, I thought.

Patsy adjusted to Colorado life somewhat slowly. She couldn't find a store that sold the right makeup and lipstick, which, she said, were staples for a woman from the South. With her typical zeal, though, she became involved in everything that had to do with the community and the children: the Boulder Historical Society, the Halloween Parade on the Pearl Street Mall, organizing a school fundraiser, the Junior League, and the Annual Christmas parade, for which she designed and decorated floats for the kids. In 1995, she created a float made from a sailboat to look like the *Good Ship Lollipop*. Boy Scouts and life-sized gingerbread men marched alongside it handing out candy.

Just days before JonBenét was murdered, Patsy had her sitting atop a friend's convertible in the Christmas parade waving at the people lining the streets. Patsy's mother told me later that a strange man approached the car during the parade and it made her uncomfortable. I think about these things now and it makes me cringe. We were so naïve. I now believe with all my heart that it's not a good idea to put your child on public display. When I think about the 1996 Christmas season and the events leading up to it, my mind wonders about the party in our home for 150 people on the thirteenth, JonBenét performing in the Colorado Little Miss Christmas Pageant on the seventeenth, the kids in the Children's Christmas Parade, the party on the twenty-third in our home, a strange 911 call made from our home on the twenty-third, JonBenét's friend telling her mother that JonBenét had told her Santa had promised a special visit to her after Christmas. All this without the burglar alarm working, a broken window in the basement, and blindly trusting all was well.

A killer was out there in the dark.

And he is *still* out there.

In late 1991, Lockheed bought 25 percent of our business in their attempt to diversify into commercial markets. We continued to grow under Lockheed, opened offices in Europe, and our annual sales reached five hundred million dollars. Yet as

I told you, I was a worrier. I never felt we had made it. I thought of the competition, and by comparison, we were small potatoes. Access Graphics hit the billion-dollar sales mark on December 15, 1996. That morning I stood at the door and shook hands with each person as they came to work. Hitting the billion-dollar mark was a terrific milestone for our employees. They had made it possible. On December sixteenth, we organized a celebration at the Hotel Boulderado with a sumptuous buffet lunch for our employees. It was a happy time, a time to be thankful, a time to celebrate.

But there was one ominous moment for me when I learned our advertising department had contacted the newspaper to announce our success. I heard about it and immediately felt a sharp twinge in my gut. Maybe that wouldn't be a good idea to announce publicly that we had just hit the billion-dollar sales mark. But since the enthusiasm was so high in the office, I overrode my gut feeling and didn't object. (Besides, my pride crept in and I really didn't mind if the world knew what we had accomplished.) The local newspaper ran a story on us quoting me as president of the company along with my photograph. Later I would wonder if such publicity had drawn the attention of the killer, who might hate big business, Access Graphics, or Lockheed.

I keep mulling over that December of 1996. I go over and over it in my mind. The Christmas parties, the friends, JonBenét's performance in the High Peaks Elementary School program, and her appearance in the Christmas program at Southwest Plaza Mall. Then that Boulder Christmas Parade with both Burke and JonBenét participating. And there was Santa, the children's parties, the twilight service at St. John's Church, and the children's party at our house—and oh God, Christmas Day.

I don't know what drew the attention of the killer. Was it the pageants? Was it at her dance lessons? Was she watched while playing in the neighborhood? Was it the newspaper article?

How do I feel about child pageants? I think you'll understand why I tell you, I do not like them. Patsy and JonBenét engaged in them strictly for fun and mother-daughter time. Patsy would laugh, "It would be good if JonBenét *lost* some of these contests. She needs to understand that you don't win all the time in life!"

It never occurred to Patsy for a minute that we might be putting our child in harm's way by entering her in the pageants. Her mother and sisters saw JonBenét as a future Miss America. They helped coach and train her and created her costumes and hairstyles for the competitions. Pageants were something Patsy and her family were familiar with, enjoyed, and were experienced in. Both Patsy and her sister Pam won the Miss West Virginia title on different years. They had participated in beauty pageants since junior high school when growing up in Parkersburg, West Virginia.

Patsy had never forgotten the thrill of her participation in the Miss America Pageant. She took JonBenét with her to a Miss West Virginia reunion in 1993, and after seeing her mother onstage, JonBenét wanted to be just like her. She was an extroverted child and simply loved performing. She took part in her first dance recital held at the Boulder High School theater, tap dancing with four other little tappers and singing to the Beatles' recording of "I Want to Hold Your Hand." Watching her from the front row, I was flabbergasted. "Good Heavens, where'd she ever learn how to do that?" I asked Patsy, who sat there beaming.

It was not an easy time for Patsy. She still had the cancer threat looming over her, and she wanted to have something special she and JonBenét shared, something she could teach and give to her daughter. And besides, she didn't know how much time she had left.

"John, pageants are a good opportunity for little girls to learn poise and to develop their talents. It'll be our mother-daughter experience she'll always remember."

They sang the song from the musical *Gypsy,* with lyrics that said whatever they did, wherever they went, they were "gonna go through it together," and for Patsy, JonBenét was more than a daughter, she was her little buddy. JonBenét would put on short plays for us at home, sometimes chastising us for not paying attention. She'd appear from behind a door in a dress and hat from her costume trunk and Patsy would announce, "Presenting Miss JonBenét Ramsey!"

How could I deny my girls their fun?

The media and tabloids made it seem as though JonBenét did nothing but pageants. They called her a little beauty queen. How little they knew. JonBenét was also a tomboy, she loved gymnastics and art, skating, playing in the park, hiking with Dad and Mom, playing with her brother, making crafts, and school. Life in general held a million interests for this child. Patsy had her busy taking piano and violin lessons at one time. She could stand on her head, turn somersaults, and climb trees like any boy in the neighborhood. She was signed up for rock climbing lessons in January 1997, like her brother, and could hardly wait to start. Burke told me, "Dad, JonBenét is good at rock climbing—she's like a spider!"

After Patsy's cancer was declared in remission, she wanted to make every minute count, and I could see that. I observed this with admiration because Patsy did everything with so much enthusiasm. If Patsy said she'd tackle a task, you could count on an elaborate, over-the-top job because she couldn't do anything halfway.

If I showed concern about the pageants, Patsy would ask, "Okay, tell me, what's out there for young girls to do to develop self-esteem?"

"Well, there's sports..."

"Uh-huh, sports. Boys have Little League baseball and soccer and football to build their self-confidence. What's out there for girls?"

Well, okay, I just wanted my girls to be happy.

I told JonBenét before these little pageants, "Remember, honey, it's your talent that counts. Don't worry so much about the beauty part. Concentrate on the talent part."

"Okay, Dad," and off she'd bound to play with Burke and his pals.

My biggest fear was that JonBenét would turn eighteen and run off to Hollywood. She was so friendly, so trusting...

Patsy and I again and again searched our souls asking if we did the wrong thing by allowing her to perform onstage in public. Would our child still be alive if she had not been in those child pageants?

Was the killer there all the time?

Was he watching in the audience as she sang and

danced with moms and aunts and grandmas applauding?

Was he scrutinizing and plotting from the shadows on the sidewalk during the Boulder parades as JonBenét passed, waving and grinning happily from her perch on the convertible?

Did he spot our child in the mall shopping with her mom and follow them home?

Was he sitting in church with us?

Was our sin that I was successful?

Patsy and I prayed every day for help, for guidance, for answers. Most of the time we begged.

"Lord, help!"

His answers came in the loving support of our friends. In April 1997, we were still staying with friends in Boulder so Burke could complete the fourth grade at his school. We wanted him to have some semblance of normalcy in his life, although it was almost impossible with the media frenzy still in full swing. Our friends were good enough to insist we remain with them, going out of their way to protect us and make us feel welcome and at home. To be surrounded by such kindness and concern was for us a cool compress on our fevered brows. It didn't eliminate the fever, but it provided sweet relief.

There was no area of our lives that wasn't invaded by the media. They tried tapping our telephone and intercepting our mail; they attempted to corner Burke as well as parents and teachers at his school. They trailed me as I tried returning to work, harassing my coworkers, even following me to my doctor's office. One morning when our hostess carried out the garbage to the bins behind the house, she noticed they were empty. She thought for a moment: It was garbage pickup day and the garbage truck hadn't come yet, so how could the bins be empty? Was someone stealing the garbage? Our host called the Boulder police and was told that if you put something out in the trash, it's fair game for anyone. I couldn't help snickering at the thought of some poor tabloid reporter reduced to garbage burrowing. "It must be an entry-level job," we joked. Who else could it be but someone looking for a juicy tidbit for the tabloids?

Our hosts came up with an idea to make the task quite awful, and began pouring foul-smelling fish fertilizer in every bag of garbage that went into the bins. The smell was terrible enough to cause the eyes to water. It didn't deter the thieves. Week after week the stinky garbage disappeared before the trucks came along. Some unfortunate tabloid reporter was digging through each disgusting tidbit of fish-fertilized garbage and coming up with nothing but waste, sore and stinging eyes, and a nasty smell that would last for hours.

One Saturday afternoon Patsy decided to venture outside the house, even though photographers lurked out front poised for the instant one of us made an appearance. She managed to slip out with Burke through the back door and dart across the yard unseen to the car. She felt a welcome sense of relief at being able to dodge the cameras and looked forward to enjoying the afternoon like a normal mother and son. They stopped at the supermarket to do a little shopping and at the checkout counter our boy saw the headlines of one of the tabloids: JONBENÉT'S BROTHER DID IT!

Burke's face fell, his eyes watering. "Mom?"

Patsy knelt with her arms around him, the afternoon ruined. "Son, don't you pay any attention to what they're saying. They are not very nice people." Still, how was he to forget the picture of his little sister on the cover of the tabloid with such a devastating headline? Who were these people doing this to his family and his sister?

We weren't quite sure how Burke managed the realization that his sister was gone, that she was in Heaven and wouldn't be coming back.

When the police interrogated him, they asked him what made him the saddest. He said, "My sister won't get to play with all her Christmas presents."

CHAPTER 11

Trusting God

Trust in the LORD with all your heart,
And lean not on your own understanding;
In all your ways acknowledge Him,
And He shall direct your paths.
—Proverbs 3:5–6

C. S. Lewis writes about moral conscience, about the knowledge of right and wrong. He argues in his writings that this basic knowledge of right and wrong is ingrained in our hearts as an absolute truth. We don't abstain from murder because it is against the law. We abstain from it because we just *know* it's wrong. This "built-in" knowledge of right and wrong was evidence to Lewis that God exists. Where else could this awareness of good and right come from?

I'm a logical-thinking engineer—I've been taught you have to prove something for it to be right. A hypothesis must be proven or disproven. As I began to mature, I was constantly looking for the proofs of God's existence. As I opened myself up to study, read, think, and analyze, I couldn't find anything logical that *disproved* the existence of God. Archeology continues to support the Bible as a historically accurate document. For me, faith in a real, living God was gradual. Some people have a lightning bolt moment; I did not. My faith journey was first a logical exercise that challenged doubt, then my mind was satisfied, and then my faith transferred to my heart, where I no longer felt the need to look for proof.

I think about the resurrection of Christ and think, as a logical person, if I had been there as one of the original disciples of Jesus, what could have happened to give me such a powerful, unshakable faith that I would go to my death rather than deny Him? The only reasonable answer to me is that these disciples had to witness Jesus put to death and then later saw Him resurrected and alive, as the Bible describes. The disciples saw him die, saw his body carried off to the tomb, and then they saw him walking the earth again—for *forty* days. It had to be something that dramatic for them to go to their deaths rather than deny that Jesus was Who He said He was. That realization makes the resurrection very believable to me.

The Apostle Paul didn't witness Jesus walking the earth after He had risen from the dead. I didn't witness Jesus walking the earth either after He was crucified or laid in a tomb. And I didn't have a Damascus road experience like Paul, but the Bible tells us we're given the gift of faith by His Spirit. We can't just decide to have faith. It's a gift. In my case, I had to challenge the gift of faith by reasoning and questioning, and it finally passed the test.

My father was a decorated World War II pilot and was awarded the Distinguished Flying Cross. He not only taught me about airplanes, but taught me by his example what it meant to be a man and the head of a household. He was the best pilot I've ever known, and he was also a man who was a great father figure. When we moved from Nebraska to Michigan, he worked for the state government and became heavily involved in aviation and building airports. He worked hard, and he taught my brother, Jeff, and me the principles he lived by. "Maintain your integrity, boys, work hard, there is nothing you can't do if you set your mind to it."

He was a big man, over six feet tall, and rugged. He played college football and Jeff followed his footsteps onto the football field as a high school quarterback. I was too small to play football and too short for basketball, but my father never made me feel bad because I didn't follow him in sports. I ran track and cross-country, and I made the school wrestling team, and Dad was right there encouraging me on. He wasn't one to tell me he loved me or give me hugs, but I knew he did love me and was very proud of me.

We grew up around airplanes, and when we were kids, Dad let us fly alongside him as his copilots. He was a patient teacher. Jeff and I often flew with him in a Twin Cessna 310 or a Twin Beechcraft 18, and he would let us work the radios and put down the landing gear when we came in for landings. We followed his directions with an overwhelming sense of responsibility, thrilled to be doing something so important. While our friends were busy with earthbound activities like riding bikes and flying kites, Jeff and I were high above the earth being copilots in our dad's airplane. Thanks to him, we both had our pilot's licenses before we left home.

Years later when I had an airplane of my own,

my children took turns sitting beside me in the copilot's seat. I could see the same delight and excitement on their faces that I'd felt as a boy as they learned how to work the radios and be in charge of letting down the landing gear. Eventually Burke would receive his pilot's license, and I hope one day he, too, will have the joy of his children copiloting beside him.

It's a fabulous experience to sit in the cockpit of an airplane with the surrounding sky like crystal-clear water, the clouds above and below like pieces of surreal puffed cotton, the steady hum of the engines; headphones in place, hand on the yoke, and the earth with all its troubles far, far below. A sense of tranquillity and single focus takes over as you soar through the molecules of air above the earth in a journey that brings you a little closer to God.

When I told my dad I had volunteered for Navy Officer Candidate School at the age of twenty-one during the Vietnam War, I saw the conflicted look on his face. He was proud of me for volunteering to serve my country, but he worried about my getting sent to combat. I brushed aside his concerns. I didn't understand the unconditional love a parent has for a child and the overpowering instinct to protect. I felt it wasn't right for me to shirk my responsibility by getting a draft deferment, which

I could have done because of my engineering degree. I had a job offer from a government agency to work as an electrical engineer, and with the offer letter was a form to fill out for a draft deferment.

It didn't feel right.

Perhaps since my dad was a war hero, I couldn't just skip off to Canada with a flower in my teeth, or take the government job to get out of going into the service. Nobody wanted to go to Vietnam. I'm sure my dad didn't want to go to India during World War II and fly cargo missions over the Himalayas, or the Hump, as it was known. My government said the Vietnam War was a just cause, and I was going to serve my country.

I was stationed at the Subic Bay Naval Base in the Philippines and later at the Naval Air Station in Atlanta, Georgia. The Philippines was an experience I'll never forget because on the weekends I flew all over the islands in a Beechcraft T34 and felt like a true Indiana Jones character. I served on active duty for three-and-a-half years and in the Reserves after that for four years. I left the active duty reserves with the rank of lieutenant commander. I still feel proud and get the chills when I hear the Navy's "Anchors Aweigh" played at concerts.

One day while stationed at the Air Station in Atlanta, I received a telephone call from our base chaplain. I felt somewhat honored that he'd call me, and when he asked if he could pay a visit, I agreed. At last somebody to talk with about God. Maybe the chaplain would have some answers for me. I began to make a list of questions for him. For example, why do Christians believe the only way to God is through Jesus? And do we go straight to Heaven when we die, or do we go to Purgatory first? Do angels really exist?

The chaplain arrived with his wife, enthusiastic about the purpose of his visit. We sat in the small living room of our second-floor apartment, and just as I thought we might get into some serious spiritual discussion, he pulled out an Amway catalog and began selling me on the benefits of becoming an Amway distributor. The evening ensued without a word about God, the Bible, Jesus, or the afterlife. I didn't become an Amway distributor, but I did buy a bottle of rug cleaner from him, which I never used. I can still see his face in my living room and hear his voice, "Why, you can make up to five thousand dollars a month in your spare time, Lieutenant! Think of it!" It gave me a feeling not unlike discovering I'd taken the wrong train and was already halfway to nowhere. Once again my spiritual journey was derailed. My Bible questions would have to wait.

I wanted to be like my dad when I became a father. With the birth of my first child, I immediately understood the unique love a parent has for a child. With the arrival of each child after Beth, I realized afresh the magnitude of the name *Father,* and it became a priority for me to fulfill this role the best I could—to be the kind of father my children could be as proud of. When I think of God's love for us, I realize I am His child and He loves me, just as I love my children—unconditionally.

Imagine my feelings when, in 1999, a Christian television program introduced Patsy and me as "The Most Hated Couple in the World." Thankfully, neither my mom nor my dad lived to see that day, but my children did! Each of my children was subpoenaed to appear and testify before a grand jury and explain the conduct of their parents, who were under suspicion of murder. I desperately wanted to protect them from this assault, but I was powerless. Imagine our twelve-year-old child, Burke, having to testify before a grand jury. Imagine Melinda, who was five months pregnant, having to travel to Boulder to testify before a hostile prosecutor. I learned that John Andrew was treated very harshly by the prosecutor when he testified. I was angry about the treatment of my children, but could do nothing to change things or help them. I knew, however, that they would represent our family well.

I was supposed to be the big, strong dad who protected his family from harm. The claws of persecution burrowed into everything I held near, dear, and valuable. The day-to-day pain of loss sometimes was almost too intense to bear. I loved each of my children as much as I loved JonBenét. I had to be strong for them, for Patsy, no matter how shredded and painful my life had become. The pain of losing our JonBenét hurt us as much as we could be hurt—the police and media assaults were insignificant by comparison.

No matter how much time passed, I would still carry that unbearable knowledge that my helpless six-year-old baby was murdered while I slept. Why didn't I hear a noise and wake up? Why didn't I come to her rescue? That's what dads are supposed to do! I would have given my life for her in an instant. Why wasn't she still alive and with us right now and the attacker in prison or dead because I got to her on time—because I rescued her *on time?*

Beth's death was an accident, and I had to accept that accidents do happen in life, but JonBenét was willfully *murdered*. Her death had been planned and calculated, and was no accident. This is something so inconceivable, so unthinkable. Murdered? Surely we were dreaming. Surely I'd wake up from this nightmare with our child still peacefully asleep in her bed, safe and secure.

And here it is, Christmas again.

Is that our youngest child scampering up the stairs, ponytail bobbing, calling, "Merry Christmas, Mommy! Merry Christmas, Daddy!"

Oh no.

Merry Christmas.

I have a recurring nightmare in which I'm flying a small single-engine plane and I suddenly come upon a high mountain range. Somehow I must cross over it, but I'm afraid I'll be unable to gain enough altitude in the small airplane, which has reached its climb performance limit. I don't think I can make it and I'll crash into the mountainside. Small piston-engine airplanes lose power and lift with higher and higher altitudes. Eventually there's not enough power to move the airplane through the air fast enough to produce more lift than the force of gravity, and the airplane can't climb anymore. My nightmare always involves the same mountain range that I need to traverse, and as I approach this impossible obstacle to cross, I always miraculously slide over to safety with only a few feet between me and the mountain peak and then I descend on the back side of the range with the rest of my journey assured. The threat is behind me. I made it over the mountain. This nightmare is so real that when I wake up, it takes me a few seconds to realize I'm not in a cockpit, but I'm at home in my bed.

Now that I understand a little more about

dreams, I see that this life-threatening dream has a message. After all, I do make it over an insurmountable obstacle even though the aircraft is ill-equipped. The journey home is assured when I get past the part that seems impossible to survive. I believe God gave me this dream to teach me to trust Him and to encourage me to go on, even though I feel spiritually ill-equipped and unprepared to get beyond life's treacherous mountain peaks. In the dream, I do make it to the other side, the other side of suffering, and the other side is peaceful and safe. I hold on to this dream to lift me up when I'm especially discouraged.

I've flown in bad weather, particularly in the summer months when afternoon and evening thunderstorms are frequently a threat. Usually they're pop-up thunderstorms that can be circumnavigated, but sometimes they appear as a huge wall and can cause any pilot stress and uncertainty. One summer morning after I had just gotten my instrument rating, I flew from Atlanta to Knoxville, Tennessee, for a business meeting. It was a beautiful, clear morning. After a full day of work in Knoxville, I was eager to get back home, but there were storms brewing over the Smoky Mountains between Knoxville and Atlanta. If I was going to get home that night, I had to pass through a very powerful group of thunderstorms that formed a thick wall across my intended flight path. This was before storm scopes, real-time Nexrad weather cockpit radar displays, or even the Weather Channel.

I walked over to the Departure Control Center before taking off to look at the storms on their radar. I figured I'd be able to form a visual image of the magnitude of the storm wall better that way and decide whether to go or spend the night in Knoxville. As I stood looking at the radar sweep, the controller was quite confident as he pointed out the narrow path between and around cells that would get me through the storm wall.

"Mr. Ramsey, you should be able to get through right here," he told me, pointing out the one clear, but crooked path through the line of storms. "The storms haven't moved much, so that path ought to stay open." I agreed that it seemed doable, but the controller would have to guide me. I would have no way of finding this path once airborne, as my plane was not equipped with radar. It was easy for him to treat the situation so calmly, but I started to sweat.

"Okay," I said, "but remember, I've got a family."

He laughed. "No problem. Tell the missus to put the coffee on."

With my newly acquired instrument flight rating, I was naïve about the threat of big thunderstorms. A wiser choice would have been to wait until morning when the storms would have dissipated. But I was young, inexperienced in dealing with weather, and I wanted to get home.

I took off trusting an unfamiliar controller to guide my small airplane and me. I climbed out in the dark night sky made even darker and more threatening by the surrounding thunderstorms and lightning that illuminated the rain on both sides of my small plane. I could only rely on my eyes, the controller talking to me via radio, and an Automatic Direction Finder to avoid the storms. My simple ADF needle dutifully pointed to the lightning strikes outside the rain-streaked cockpit windows, but I knew the ADF performed imperfectly at best.

Remembering the image on the controller's radar screen, I knew there was a point at which I must make a turn to the right or I would fly into a storm cell in front of me and be torn to pieces. This turn would be key to my safe passage, and only the controller knew when I should make that turn. He was the one watching the blip on his radar that was my small airplane and my life. No airplane, large or small, flies through a mature thunderstorm because they're just too powerful. I had to completely trust the controller for guidance.

The controller had been quiet and the thought struck me that maybe he had left his post. Maybe he'd gone on a break, or maybe his shift was over. Just as I really began to sweat, his voice came through the radio giving me the instruction, "Baron 88Juliet, turn right to a heading of 250." That was what I was waiting for. Clear guidance. I turned and soon was on the back side of the thunderstorm line.

I trusted the controller that menacing night with my life. His voice was calm, reassuring, and he was right there with me in danger. It was an unforgettable life lesson in understanding the concept of trusting God with my life. I had to realize my powerlessness and desperate need for the Lord's perfect guidance.

I believe only God knows the path we should take through life's storms, and my challenge and responsibility is to trust Him, the way I trusted the controller that night. I don't want to live my life in a panic, white-knuckling every crack of thunder as I did that night in the storm. The controller's voice was quietly confident. Maybe I could learn to remember that God's voice is calm, and even though He may be silent at times, He's always there, watching, caring, ready to guide us away from the paths that might devastate our souls.

If there's one thing I want you to gain from

reading this book, it's understanding that *tragedy doesn't have to damage our souls.* I realize only too well that I could spend the rest of my life bitter, wounded, grieving, sad, angry—but these emotions lead nowhere. I must believe that God, in His kind, gentle, and caring manner, is right beside me, guiding and loving me through the extreme pain I've been subject to.

If I totally trust God, which isn't always easy to surrender to, I know I'll be guided through the storms of life to a safe passage and achieve "the peace of God, which surpasses all understanding" (Philippians 4:7). It would take absolute trust.

CHAPTER 12

All Things for Good?

*God judged it better to bring good out of evil
than to suffer no evil to exist.*
—St. Augustine

There's a refrain in the eighteenth-century French opera *L'Arlésienne*, by Bizet, "I envy the shepherd who sleeps." It's true that when fear or sorrow overtakes us, a good night's sleep is almost impossible to come by. At some point we really must sleep. For a while after Beth's death, I couldn't bring myself to sleep in a bed. I felt I should honor her by the act of discomfort and sleep on the floor. For weeks, I lay on the floor beside the bed, my face in my hands, my heart aching. When

JonBenét was murdered, I hit the floor again. Sleep wouldn't come, and when it did, it was fitful. I refused to sleep in the comfort of a bed. Making myself comfortable just didn't seem right.

The friends we stayed with insisted we eat. Eat? How do you chew and taste anything when you're in mourning? How do you sit before a plate with your knife and fork and think about swallowing something? Loving friends brought casseroles, salads, cakes, and snacks to the house for us. The meals stacked up in the kitchen overflowing the counters. Patsy was worse off than I, and getting her to eat was almost impossible. At least I managed a cracker and a cup of soup.

Anyone who is going through a traumatic experience must be mindful of his or her health. And let me say, the traumatic experience doesn't have to be the death of a child. It can be a divorce, loss of a job, children leaving home, a bad diagnosis, the breakup of a relationship—anything that emotionally clobbers you. When we're suffering emotionally with our hearts broken and our world turned upside down, we don't care about things like eating, getting proper sleep, or exercising. I'll wager you've never heard of a person in mourning who leaps into their running shoes and heads out for a three-mile run, then comes back to whip up a power protein drink in the blender while tossing down vitamin and mineral tablets. No, it's more common that we completely lose interest in our health. We simply don't care, and the last thing we concern ourselves with is exercising or eating right.

Eventually, we *must* care. It's a step toward survival and recovery. Eat regular, healthy meals and take vitamin supplements for no other reason than you *must*. I tried to eat to be polite, and that was motivation enough to get some nourishment. Patsy ultimately did the same, trying to be gracious and not hurt anyone's feelings. There she sat, draped in grief, and smiling a thoughtful smile of gratitude at a kindly neighbor spooning chicken cacciatore on good china dishes for us.

Sleep is important as a restorative process, and for both Patsy and me, it was also an escape. In sleep the living nightmare of what had happened to our little girl would go away for a while. Our minister advised us to get up in the morning, deal with the day at hand for as long as we could, and when we couldn't handle the day any longer, to take a Benadryl or Ambien tablet and go to bed. Our doctors concurred.

Which brings me to the subject of medication. When going through a trauma, medication can be a blessing. I advise people not to resist taking medication during this time. It's doubtful you'll become a drug addict, and you're not defying the power of God to restore you. Get a prescription if the over-the-counter medication doesn't help. If you broke your leg, you'd wear a splint. Your heart is broken now and you need help.

Time is one of God's tools for healing, and medication can help during trauma or grief. When JonBenét died, both Patsy and I were put under the care of a doctor who prescribed medication for a while. It didn't erase the grieving, but it helped ease the razor-sharp slashes of anguish that rendered us irretrievably helpless.

Speaking of medication, a friend told us a funny story about herself after the death of a grandfather, whom she hardly knew. She was one of those proud, sanctified souls who never took medication other than novocaine at the dentist's if she had a cavity. This girl didn't drink coffee or tea, had never tasted liquor, and rarely even took an aspirin. Conscientious to a fault, she thought it only proper to show up for this funeral even though the grandfather was a virtual stranger. As she was boarding the plane, a well-meaning friend, thinking she was probably in deep grief, gave her Valium, a mild tranquilizer. She swallowed it and instantly conked out, and didn't wake up until three days later. She was helped off the plane by flight attendants, and she could barely sit up through the funeral, the grave service, and the reception following. The family still laughs about it because she was present through it all, propped up on chairs, sitting at the table, riding in the car, parked on sofas, while snoozing away.

My point is, be aware of what medication you are taking and don't be afraid to sleep whenever you want. If you normally sleep eight hours a night, it's okay to sleep ten to twelve hours a night. You're not lazy, you're hurting. I know how easy it is for a person's spirit to break and remain broken after tragedy strikes. We work tirelessly to build good, happy, and productive lives, and then tragedy strikes, and like a delicate house of cards, everything comes crashing down. And we forget about taking care of ourselves.

Besides eating healthy food, we need exercise. We need to stir up our endorphins. Get outdoors and go for a walk with a friend. Patsy, Burke, and I lived shrouded behind locked doors and covered windows twenty-four hours a day with the media lurking outside. We had to be quite inventive to sneak out for a walk without being photographed. If you don't have a dozen cameras pointed at you with reporters yelling out inflammatory and insulting remarks, you should be able to head outdoors and put one foot in front of the other and take a walk every day for thirty minutes or so.

Finally, know you're not alone. It dawned on me that I had been living my life without being truly involved with God. I recognize now that I can actually have a *relationship* with God, and it's the most important one of my life.

No matter where you are and what's happening around you, you're not alone. God knows all, sees all, and He's there with you. I'm still realizing this, and it gives me a profound sense of peace, confidence, and most important, hope.

In the movie *The Shawshank Redemption*, Morgan Freeman plays a man sentenced to life in prison. He says from his prison cell, "Hope is a dangerous thing in here. It can drive a man crazy." What he's saying is that hope is the anticipation of a better future, but for someone sentenced to life in prison, how can there be a better future? You feel the same way when you've lost something or someone precious to you. Imprisoned with a life sentence, and hopeless. But eventually, hope emerges. In time I'd see that God had a purpose for my life, just as He had a purpose for JonBenét's short life. I'd see it and I'd believe it.

However, as the months passed, Patsy and I remained involuntary actors in the international entertainment industry. We seemed to be material for every newscast, talk show, and gossip column. The media had portrayed me as a real life J. R. Ewing, the wealthy, evil character in the old TV series *Dallas*. Patsy was made out to be spoiled and cunning, more selfish and mean than the witch in *The Wizard of Oz*.

In 1998, Howard Rosenberg, a *Los Angeles Times* columnist, wrote, "The still-unsolved slaying of JonBenét Ramsey has initiated one of the foulest, yellowest chapters in contemporary U.S. journalism." (See Rosenberg's full story in the Appendix.)

Most debilitating to us wasn't the attack of the media and the allegations by the Boulder police. I'll say it again. It was the loss of our child. We were shattered by the loss of our child.

Years after JonBenét was murdered, a media watchdog publication would note that there were more print lines about JonBenét's death than Princess Diana's tragedy. The article also reported that the media had generated more than a billion dollars in revenue from pursuing our story. The headline on the magazine that month was JONBENÉT, INC.: A BILLION DOLLAR INDUSTRY.

No, life isn't always fair.

CHAPTER 13

God's Promises

*The LORD is near to all who call upon Him,
To all who call upon Him in truth.*
—Psalm 145:18

The children's party at our house with the Santa Claus we hired was in full swing. Santa, stroking his beard and chuckling, played his part perfectly.

"Does Christmas come just once a year?" he asked.

"Yeeees," they all cheered at once.

He asked another question. "And who can tell me where Christmas lives the rest of the year?"

Silence. Then JonBenét raised her hand and

pointed to her heart. "In here," she said. "Christmas lives in here. With Jesus."

I remember admiring our Christmas tree with its dozens of sparkling lights. I remember the happy chatter of children. I remember the candy, the gingerbread houses. I remember, "Jesus lives in here."

All light pales in the presence of the true Light, the Light that lives "in here."

The true Christian is indwelled with light, the light of God. JonBenét, six years old, knew that.

I've come to realize that no matter how blessed or privileged a person might be, we are each forced at one time or another to walk through the valley of suffering. It comes as a surprise to us, this valley. We can't figure out why we're plunged into such a dark place.

After JonBenét's death, I was deep in my dark valley, and my older children, John Andrew and Melinda, tried to be a comfort to me, in spite of their own pain. Melinda is quiet like me, yet a very strong woman. She didn't discuss the strain and pressure being exerted on her own family, but called regularly to assure and encourage me with her loving concern.

John Andrew was especially protective of me. He was with us at our lake home in Charlevoix when the paparazzi descended on us like hungry crows with their cameras, cell phones, and note pads. A local bar became their hangout in the evenings, and John Andrew happened to be in that very bar one night and overheard several tabloid photographers bad-mouthing our family. His indignation reached its limit, and he told the men that it was his family they were talking about and to knock it off, or leave. One of the guys became belligerent but John Andrew stood his ground. The bar owner threw the reporter and his cronies out.

John Andrew didn't say a word about the incident when he came home later that night. The next day we received a huge bouquet of fresh flowers from the bar owner with an apology. We couldn't figure out why we would get flowers from a local bar. We were baffled.

"What in the world do you suppose this is for?" Patsy puzzled.

John Andrew looked a bit sheepish. "Well, um, you see, uh, last night—" He told us what happened with the reporters, that he had stuck up for his family and it caused a ruckus.

Light spread into my valley that day through my son. My son had stood up and defended us. For a father, that's a wonderful feeling. God had not left us alone. It's so important to beware of becoming accustomed to the dark. The longer we sit crouched in the night of our soul, the more likely we are to accept darkness as our fate. The valley becomes our address, our souls stay solemn and wounded, and we begin making choices to accommodate our misery.

We human beings were born with a built-in desire to seek God. For C. S. Lewis this was another proof of God's existence, because God does not give us a desire for something that cannot be fulfilled.

In the Bible, nearly all the heroes of the faith were thrust into valleys of suffering, yet they trusted God, who empowered them *within* to endure the darkness of their valleys and overcome suffering with courage and dignity.

I was learning when we stay close to God, we can withstand and overcome the most intense suffering. I observed the burdens of the believers in India, where persecution was imminent at all times. One Indian pastor told me, his black eyes glistening, "They can burn down the church, but they can't burn down our faith. We stay strong by staying close to the Lord Jesus."

It was by reading the scriptures and spending time in prayer that I came to discover we can become one with God's heart and mind. The material world loses its grip on our thoughts. I heard a testimony of a man who said that during the darkest period in his life, he felt closer to God than he ever had before, and now that he was out of the dark valley of suffering, he missed that unique closeness to God he had experienced. He said he'd almost welcome more suffering so he could feel that closeness again.

I thought about that.

I, too, am discovering a sense of profound peace, and I feel closer to God than ever before in my life. I'm amazed at how my prayers are becoming prayers of gratitude and no longer sorrowful imprecations for help.

Romans 8:28 says that "all things work together for good to those who love God," but if you had told me these words at the time of JonBenét's death, I would have thought you were grossly insensitive. How could something good come out of the murder of a sweet, innocent baby?

There's the story of Joseph in the Bible. His cruel, jealous brothers threw him in a pit and then sold him as a slave to foreigners. From this hopeless situation, Joseph rose to be the number two man in Egypt, the most powerful nation in the known world, under the Pharaoh himself. In this exalted position, earned through years of suffering, including imprisonment, he had the means and influence to preserve the entire Hebrew race by providing land and homes for them in the land of Goshen. He told his shocked brothers as he forgave them, with his arms outstretched, "But as for you,

you meant evil against me; *but* God meant it for good" (Genesis 50:20).

When I read those words, I claimed them for myself. I prayed, "Lord, let it be so with me. What the devil meant for evil, You will turn to good."

Patsy and I had several opportunities to see those words come alive in our lives. We saw God take what man had meant to harm us and turn it around for good. A marginal attorney sued us on behalf of a convicted sex offender for naming him as someone the police needed to look at. His former girlfriend came forward and said she was absolutely convinced he had murdered JonBenét. Not to pay attention to this information would have been foolish. I believe the lawsuit was meant to harass us and gain some national publicity for the attorney, who was able to appear on the *Today Show*, *The O'Reilly Factor*, and other national programs to discuss his suit.

A federal judge in Atlanta dismissed the lawsuit after reviewing the evidence thoroughly, and wrote a ninety-three-page opinion which stated that the preponderance of the evidence indicated an intruder had entered our home that night and murdered JonBenét. It was the first time someone of high authority in the justice system looked at the evidence and publicly supported our innocence. This ray of light for us extended well beyond just the dismissal of a lawsuit. It spoke to us that God was faithful. God saw the intention to harm us with accusations and He turned it around to give us a highly reputable articulation of justice.

I would not have chosen to learn about God's faithfulness the way I did, but I want to share with you as openly as I can what God has done in me through it all. It was an awareness of His faithfulness that pulled me out of a hole of despair and gave me the foundation for hope for the future.

In 2002, Patsy's regular medical checkup showed the cancer had returned, after nine years in remission. I tried to reassure her, "We'll beat this thing, darling. We'll beat this."

She had developed deep faith in the Lord, and even as she lay in the hospital half alert while undergoing more chemotherapy, she praised and worshipped God. Her gentle face strained by stress, Patsy praised the Lord.

"I know You're here with me, Lord...I thank you, Lord, for being here with me through this..."

I became a believer in a faithful God not because He answered my prayers, and not because things were going well, but rather because I began to see His presence in my life. I recognized Him as the source of inner strength. God never promised to protect us from trouble; in fact, He warns us in the Bible that life will have plenty of troubles. What He does promise is to strengthen us from the inside and bring us through the trouble.

Now this.

The cancer had returned.

In those dark days immediately following JonBenét's murder, Patsy and I would wake up in the mornings with our stomachs twisted and wonder, "What bomb is going to go off in our life today?" It became obvious to me that we had to change our expectations. Our attention had been fixed on gloom and disaster, and when I studied the Bible more carefully, I saw how we are warned about the demonic, about Satan. I didn't really understand much about an entity called Satan before my experience in India. When people would mention the devil, I used to envision a little guy in a red suit and a tail running around jabbing people with a pitchfork, as you see in the comics.

I will say with conviction that I now believe there is a spiritual realm, and there is a demonic side to that realm. Of this I now have no doubt. I didn't hear much about the demonic realm from the pulpits of churches I attended, but the Bible clearly warns us that our fight is not against people, or flesh and blood, but "against principalities, against powers, against the rulers of the darkness of this age, against spiritual *hosts* of wickedness..." (Ephesians 6:12).

The good news is, Jesus gives us power in His name over Satan's influence and actions.

Once I understood this truth, I began to push against and resist the devil's intentions to destroy me. He had already robbed me of enough. I had an injured and exhausted soul, and I began proclaiming, "Enough!"

I had to stop focusing only on our problems. I had to make peace with what was happening to us, the memory of my child's dead body, her little arms tied over her head, her mouth taped closed forever. I had to let go of my child's brutal murder, and abandon my hopeless outlook for my future.

How could I reach a point where I'd listen for the voice of God and recognize His continued faithfulness, even with the return of Patsy's cancer, and have hope for the future? I learned that we can hear the voice of God if we prepare ourselves to listen. Quiet time in conversation with God. Praying and listening. When I would train new salespeople for my business, I would tell them, if you are talking more than your customer, you are talking too much. I began to converse with God as I would with a very trusted friend. He is there with us. He won't forsake us, and He is faithful when we are not.

The Hebrew word for faith is *aman*. It means belief, assurance, trust, steadfastness, continuance. God is all of those and more. No wonder Job could exclaim for generations to hear, "Though He slay me, yet will I trust Him" (Job 13:15).

I believe God is faithful. I know that which the devil intends for evil, God will turn to good.

I thought a lot about people who lose their faith when tragedy strikes. Do we only acknowledge God when life is going along well? Can a person lose their faith in God when bad things happen in their lives? Yes, sadly, they can.

Patsy's suffering returned almost immediately with the return of cancer in 2002, but her faith grew through her suffering and disappointment. She simply refused to feel sorry for herself. I thought of my mother, who had faithfully escorted my brother and me to church as kids to give us a good spiritual foundation. Then later she rejected God, turned away from Him, and lost her faith! It bothered me for years until that night I told you about in the summer of 1980 at Lake Mecosta when I saw the shooting star. I had asked God for a sign that my mom was in Heaven; I asked for a shooting star. There it was, zinging across the night sky.

I was in the ninth grade when I first met Jon Jones, a boy my age who lived down the shoreline from our summer cottage at Lake Mecosta. My mother loved him like a son and thought for sure he would be an asset to the world someday, a young man destined for success, and everyone agreed. Jon was an all-American boy, and kind to a fault.

Jon had an uncle who had a small float plane, which he flew to a cabin he had built on a remote fishing lake far up in Canada, and one summer he invited Jon and me to come up to fish. We were so thrilled you would have thought we'd been invited to have lunch with President Kennedy. We packed up our fishing gear and made the eight-hour drive into southern Ontario, ending with a two-hour drive along a dirt road through dense pine forests to Uncle Sonny's cabin. The next day, we climbed aboard his small Piper float plane, and flew farther up into northern Canada to a remote lake.

Uncle Sonny dropped us off on an island in the middle of a pristine aqua green lake surrounded by a thick wall of pines and home to millions of mosquitoes. We were set for two days of fabulous fishing, Jon and I, outfitted with our tent, fishing poles, frying pan, matches, candy bars, flashlights, and mosquito repellant. We watched Uncle Sonny's plane take off and disappear, leaving us on our own, and I had my first taste of true isolation. The roar of the small engine vanished into the late afternoon sky. and we became surrounded by numbing silence.

In the next two days we stood on the rocky banks of that island and cast our red devil spinners out into the water and caught more northern pike than we could count. We ate a few, frying them in butter, and the rest we released back into the lake. Chewed up by mosquitoes, we weren't sad when we heard Uncle Sonny's plane humming toward us to take us back to civilization.

Over the next summers, Jon's mom and my mom each "adopted" the other boy, so we moved between cottages as if each were our own home. My mom affectionately referred to Jon as her third son. We continued to be close friends after high school graduation, and eventually he married one of the few cute girls at Lake Mecosta. They promptly had three children and I figured he had an ideal life, a good wife, great kids, and a great job at Dow Chemical. Like my mom, I still believed Jon was destined for long life and greatness.

I was wrong.

Early one summer morning, leaving his wife and kids at home, Jon and Uncle Sonny returned to that same remote lake where we had fished as boys. After fishing for a couple of days, they packed up to leave the island. Uncle Sonny's small Piper float plane accelerated on the water for lift-off, but it hit a submerged log. The impact threw them both hard against the instrument panel, knocking them unconscious, and as it sank, they drowned. It was Steve, Jon's brother, who found the half-submerged plane in the middle of the lake several days later.

How could this happen? Jon was a *good* guy. Good guys like Jon shouldn't die. Jon was young! He had a wife and small children. My mother grieved terribly, and his death brought her to angrily question the existence of God. After a lifetime of church attendance, she told me she had given up on Him. "If there really is a merciful and good God, he would not have let this happen." It made no sense to her.

Why am I telling you this story? Because we can abandon our faith in God in times of crisis and tragedy, as my mother did, for a time. My mom thought, as I had most of my life, that God would not let bad things happen to good people. What I learned was that God only promised to get us *through* life's difficulties.

CHAPTER 14

God Working Through People

It is better that a few guilty men go free than one innocent man be wrongly convicted.
—John Adams, second president of the United States

Patsy and I weren't the only parents to be placed under the umbrella of suspicion when their child has been murdered. The primary caregivers are always the first ones the police investigate when a child is harmed, missing, or killed. In our case, we became the *only* targets in the murder of our child, and from what we could see, the police refused to launch a vigorous all-out search for the real killer.

In 1995, a Colorado man named Mike Church was under suspicion of murdering his thirteen-year-old daughter, Heather. The real murderer, Charles Browne, happened to be a neighbor of the victim, and years after killing her, he was still living undiscovered, just a half mile from the Church home. When the police had interviewed him shortly after the girl's disappearance, they dismissed him as a suspect.

The murder became a cold case, and four years passed before a detective named Lou Smit was assigned to investigate the case. Smit tracked down Charles Browne, who finally confessed to murdering Heather with a blow to the head—after she discovered him burglarizing their home—and hiding her body. Lou suspected that Browne had killed before and continued to investigate. Browne eventually confessed to murdering over forty people in a period spanning from 1970 until his arrest.

It worries me to think how many other children the murderer of our child may have abused and/or killed before and after JonBenét. This type of criminal doesn't murder just once. I have been told that many murder cases have remained unsolved for years before the killer is at last brought to justice, and I shouldn't give up hope that one day he will be found. Sometimes it takes decades, but the killer is eventually brought to justice, but only if the police continue to look.

Nine months after JonBenét was murdered, an

intruder broke into a home a few blocks away from our Boulder home. The mother woke up and discovered the intruder leering over her eight-year-old daughter, who was asleep in her bedroom. The man, dressed in black ninja garb, fled out the bedroom window. He had entered the house while the family was away, and after the family returned home and set the burglar alarm for the night, the intruder waited silently until they went to bed before entering the girl's bedroom. The traumatized parents reported the attack to the Boulder police, and to me it sounded like the same monster who had murdered JonBenét, but the police quickly discounted the similarity.

The Boulder chief of police stated to the media, "This case isn't similar to the Ramsey case since this little girl wasn't murdered." The girl's father was interviewed on ABC and said, "The police investigators were completely uninterested in the similarities between our case and the Ramsey case."

The police weren't after JonBenét's killer; they were after Patsy and me.

New hope arrived five months after JonBenét's death in the person of Detective Lou Smit, the same man who caught Heather Dawn Church's killer. The detective from Colorado Springs was brought in by the district attorney to work on

JonBenét's case. Lou Smit was a near legend in Colorado law enforcement circles. He was responsible for putting more than two hundred killers behind bars. In a career spanning thirty years, Lou had never lost a homicide prosecution. Lou was assigned to the cold cases, and he solved 90 percent of them. Since Smit was skilled at solving murders, we prayed it wouldn't take him long to find who killed our baby. At last, a ray of light in the darkness.

We learned that Lou would drive from Colorado Springs each morning and, before going to work, stop at our old house and pray. Apparently, he often did this; go to the scene of the crime to just sit. Sit and pray. Patsy and I were eager to meet Lou and express our gratitude, so one morning we drove to 15th Street and found him sitting in his Chevrolet conversion van in front of our house.

"Mr. Smit, we're the Ramseys."

"Yes, I know," he said in his brushed steel baritone voice. "Nice to finally meet you." He invited us to climb in his van. Patsy gazed for a moment at our big Tudor house we had so lovingly renovated and began to shake at its sight. Our home now looked like a skeleton of a house, the dried remnants of Christmas 1996 still lying about the yard, the windows darkened as though evil had moved in and permanently shut out the light. The place was looped with yellow police tape, and the front door permanently shut, the welcome mat no longer welcoming. I held Patsy's trembling shoulders, lowering my head to hers. "It's okay, sweetheart. It's okay."

"Oh, John, I never want to step foot into that house again."

"Don't worry, Patsy, we won't. We'll leave as soon as Burke finishes the school year. We'll move back to Atlanta."

"Oh yes, John. Take me home to Atlanta. Please..."

Lou Smit seemed to understand our angst, and didn't say a word. He stared out the window at the quiet neighborhood and peaceful houses on the street, bicyclists peddling past, and finally he said, "I'm going to do my best to find who killed your daughter. I think I can do it, with God's help."

Patsy and I could see a confidence in this man that was tremendously reassuring. Like a wise grandfather who was going to make everything all right.

He nodded, and asked, "Do you mind if we have a word of prayer?"

It was a beautiful prayer. He prayed for us and he prayed the killer would be exposed. He prayed for God's guidance and help, and at the end Patsy and I took in deep breaths of gratitude. Here was a man of faith who hadn't lost a single homicide prosecution. He'd find this guy for sure. He was, to us, an example of God working in our life through His people.

But eighteen months later, in September 1998, Smit resigned from the district attorney's office. He said he removed himself from the case because the Boulder police and prosecutors "had developed tunnel vision and were focusing only on the Ramsey family and not on other suspects." When he first arrived, he assumed the police had good reason to believe we were guilty and told me later he expected to agree with the police conclusions, based on what he had heard in the media. After intense scrutiny, he found the police conclusion flawed, and told the police they were going down the wrong path. There was absolutely no evidence to substantiate their opinions that Patsy had killed our child and I was protecting her.

Smit's trained eye and disciplined mind saw the abundant evidence proving an intruder had entered our home and committed the crime as we slept. From that point on, he was not welcome in the police department. He was shut out from any further communication with the police detectives. Lou became frustrated and told us later he could be more effective in tracking down the killer outside the restricted confines of the district attorney's office.

He had no intention of stopping work on the case, he said. He was just going to do it on his own time.

In his resignation letter dated September 20, 1998, Lou Smit wrote: "The Ramseys did not do it. There is substantial, credible evidence of an intruder and a lack of evidence that the parents are involved."

Since Lou was no longer with the official investigation, we could meet and talk with him freely. We became friends and one day at lunch he opened his wallet. "See this?" It was a picture of JonBenét in her snowsuit tottering on a pair of skis taken on our last family vacation in Michigan.

"You carry JonBenét's picture in your wallet?"

"You bet I do. I think of her every day, John, and I'm going to find her killer."

Our hopes were buoyed by Lou Smit's continued dedication to the case. I was confident that somehow, someway, Detective Smit would bring JonBenét's killer to justice.

Meanwhile, there was still the matter of the ransom note, which was being referred to as the *War and Peace* of ransom notes, because of its length. Experts told me that with that much writing, it would be easy to conclusively match the killer's handwriting to the note. A linguistics scholar, who studied the ransom note, offered his services. The police were still accusing Patsy of writing the note despite no credible handwriting expert's supporting opinion. The linguistics scholar believed in Patsy's innocence, and wrote in a letter personally addressed to Patsy: "I know that you are innocent, know it, absolutely and unequivocally, I would stake my professional reputation on it, indeed, my faith in humanity. I believe you were an ideal mother, wise, protective, caring and truly devoted." He described the ransom note and said: "It appears to have been written by a young adult with an adolescent imagination overheated by true crime literature and Hollywood thrillers."

The expert was eager and willing to help find the real killer, but his offer of help was rejected by the police.

We had DNA evidence and Lou Smit believing in our innocence. Those were two pillars of our hope for solving the case. Most of the media had struck the gavel and proclaimed us guilty, but thank God, we had a great detective on our side who looked to God for guidance.

When your life is falling apart, you ache for a spark of encouragement. You want to be glad if encouragement comes, but you don't dare to be too heartened. Lou would continue to be a spark of encouragement and I have no doubt God put him in our lives for just that purpose.

In 2009, I had the opportunity to meet Ed Smart,

the father of Elizabeth Smart, when we both appeared on *The Oprah Show*. Ed's daughter, Elizabeth, was fourteen years old when she was abducted from her Salt Lake City bedroom in the middle of the night. I knew too well the terror that engulfed her parents that night. Elizabeth was missing for almost an entire year. The Salt Lake City police had extensively investigated Ed and his wife. Eventually they simply shelved the case.

I asked Ed, "How did you endure that year not knowing the whereabouts of your daughter—not knowing if she was alive or dead?" When we thought JonBenét had been kidnapped, the six hours that elapsed from the time we found the ransom note until the time I found her body were the most painful, terror-filled six hours of my life. Ed and his family had to endure that agony for almost a year, not knowing where their precious girl was, not knowing if she was alive or dead.

Ed paused before answering me, then looked at me with a somber expression. "John, I just had a strong impression that Elizabeth was alive and okay. I just clung to that impression and believed that she'd be found."

The gift of assurance is what enabled Ed Smart to function for those months that his daughter was missing. The story was widely publicized. Hundreds of people searched for her without success.

Her picture appeared on national television, and the whole country was on the alert. A police officer from another law enforcement district discovered her nearly a year after she had been abducted by a deranged former handyman and his wife.

I believe that her parents' faith, trusting she'd come home one day, somehow reached across the distance and became a source of strength for young Elizabeth, too. Eight years later, Elizabeth, with poise and dignity, testified in the trial of her kidnappers and told of her brutal ordeal.

There's a corollary to this story that strengthened my faith in the power of prayer. Patsy was at a weekend prayer retreat in Florida focused on healing, and as they prayed intensely the last day of the meeting, Patsy suddenly felt a strong urge to pray for Elizabeth Smart. So strong was the feeling that she interrupted the group and asked them to pray for Elizabeth. The group prayed that she would be found, asking God to open the way for the authorities to find her. The next day Patsy came home from the retreat and I mentioned, "Did you hear about Elizabeth Smart?"

She was all ears. "No. What happened?"

"She was found alive and well yesterday."

Patsy fell to her knees and shouted, "Oh, thank God!" She then told me about her strong impression the day before and what had happened in the prayer group. Patsy and her group of prayer warriors could have been praying for Elizabeth at the very moment she was found.

"Honey, that's the power of intercessory prayer," Patsy said. "All those prayers from everywhere going up for Elizabeth brought her home safe, I know it."

"I do, too," I said. It was my second exposure to the power of intercessory prayer, the first being when Patsy was healed, and I was about to learn much more.

An article about us circulated in the papers and on the Internet proclaiming that Patsy and I lived like two strangers, and our marriage appeared as some sort of business arrangement. We actually laughed out loud at that one. "Maybe when the person who wrote this is married as long as we've been, they'll realize married life isn't always like a teenage romance." Patsy laughed. "And besides, has this person ever seen us when we're alone?" She gave me a hug. "Maybe they've run out of things to say about us, darling."

"Besides," I added, "is there a prescribed way for a married couple to act when they've just lost a child and are under an umbrella of suspicion of murder?"

I've often been asked why some couples divorce after the loss of a child. I believe there are at least two significant reasons for this. The first is the tendency to assign blame. "You shouldn't have given Billy the keys to the car that night." "You shouldn't have let Suzy ride her bike alone on that busy street." It's natural to want to find blame, but we have to understand that we can't protect our children from all of life's risks. Blame is a destructive force. Second, a spouse is the other's support mechanism. When one loses their job, the spouse is there to give encouragement. When one is beaten down by the world, the other is there to help them up. When a child is lost, both husband and wife are crushed and not able to fulfill their support role to the other.

In our case, we had always been close and fortunately it seemed that when I was down, Patsy was up, and vice versa. When we were both down, we would say, "Let's stop having a pity party." It helped us recognize what was happening. After the death of JonBenét, we went to therapy and we talked about our child. Talking about her somehow kept her with us. We were the ones who loved her most in the world, and talking about her held her place in the family and our lives.

Sometimes when a loved one dies, there ensues an actual suffering competition, the idea that one person's pain is worse than another's. Patsy and I respected each other's pain. We were two hurting people needing one another's loving comfort more than ever. We went through the seven stages of grief experiencing each stage together.

First the *shock,* the disbelief, the numbness. We were in a state of shock for a long time. Then the stage of *denial*, when we kept repeating "It can't be." "This hasn't happened to us." "It's a nightmare." "Our little girl couldn't have been murdered."

Then came the stage of *bargaining.* Patsy would say, "If I go to sleep, when I wake up, I'll find out I was having a bad dream." If. If. If.

And of course, the *guilt.* The guilt stage is the longest stage because I couldn't stop blaming myself for sleeping through our child's murder, for not ensuring the burglar alarm system was on, for not checking and locking all the doors and windows before we left, for not being the protector and keeping my family safe from harm.

The *anger* stage was a big one for me because of my rage at the guy who did this unthinkable thing to our baby and at the Boulder police for their failures. Patsy's love and forgiving character tempered me and provided a balm, but I still couldn't completely shake my wrath.

The next stage, *depression,* is something we felt

almost all the time in the beginning. Our friends tried things to lift our spirits and to distract us from our misery, like one friend who always had a joke of the day for us. These jokes were sometimes so bad they were funny. Ironically, the continuous assault by the media proved to be a mental distraction that kept us focused on something other than our grief and depression. Getting Burke to and from school without being photographed became a major daily effort and gave our minds something to focus on. One heartbreaking morning Patsy stood by the door with Burke's lunch box in her hands and said to no one at all, "I keep forgetting I only have one child to get ready for school now..."

The last stage of grief is *acceptance.* This one can take years. In our case, the stages of grief I've named did not all happen in order, and some lasted longer than others. We had to understand that we'd never be the same, so we had to accept life without our child and be thankful for the years she was in our lives, and go on.

If you're a married couple and suffering the loss of a loved one, especially a child, stay close to each other, talk, share, cry, and pray together; hold on to one another with love and tenderness. You're both wounded and in deep pain. You need one another. If you're a single person, please be sure you have a special person or persons to help you through the nightmare of loss. A grief group, your pastor, a therapist, a family member, or your best friend can help; do not alienate yourself and suffer alone. The love that Patsy and I had for one another was an impenetrable fortress, as well as a refuge. When JonBenét died, Patsy and I had been married sixteen years, sixteen devoted, loving years. When tragedy exploded our peaceful life, we had each other to hang on to in the wreckage.

It's my prayer for others who experience any kind of loss that they do not alienate themselves and suffer alone. Share, cry, talk, and pray together.

Jim was a business friend of mine, the father of a fine teenage boy and a young daughter. His wife was a good woman who created a warm and inviting home. Jim was especially close to his son, who impressed me as a smart and responsible young man with a promising future. One spring afternoon in the boy's junior year of high school, he took a ride with his buddy, who had just gotten his driver's license and the keys to the family car. He climbed in the car, sharing this rite of passage with his friend, and off they went. They rounded a curve in the road, swerved, and slammed headlong into a tree. The driver came out with scratches. Jim's son was killed instantly.

Jim pulled away from people and buried himself in mourning for his son. Instead of drawing toward a place of help and healing, he pulled away from any possible hope of getting to the other side of his suffering. He built up hatred for the young driver of the car in which his son was riding. He began spending money carelessly, ignoring his wife and daughter, eventually losing his business and declaring bankruptcy. Grief was destroying him.

Grief *can* destroy us. We can mourn for years and years in a state of limbo, and our life will stay in a perpetual sinkhole. We stay trapped in darkness.

Jim finally took his own life without a thought for his little girl or his wife, who needed and loved him. His suicide was a sad statement to family and friends, giving them the message that they were not as important to him as the son he lost. Suicide always tells the living, "I don't care about you," and places a burden of guilt on them. "Why couldn't we have done something?" they are forced to ask themselves.

Was Jim's suicide a selfish act? I think so. I can't condemn him because I know what it's like to be hopeless with loss. I, too, plunged into a bottomless pit of grief and self-centeredness for a period. The person who takes his or her own life is so completely possessed with their own feelings, their own losses, problems, and troubles, that they can't perceive the feelings of anyone else. It's almost impossible to think of other people's feelings when you yourself are drowning, but there comes a time when you must. For a parent there is nothing more crushing to one's spirit than the loss of a child. I grieved the loss of both my parents, but losing a child is different from those losses—it's intensified, exaggerated, and the loss is irreplaceable. The death of a child contradicts what we believe to be normal and natural. The natural order of life has it that parents die *before* their children. When a child dies, parents feel as if they've lost their future.

People ask me how long it takes to get over the loss of a child. My response is, you never get over it. You go on as a different person—you've been deeply wounded and the scar will always be there. There's no rationalizing the death of a child. We can, and must, move on for the sake of those who are living. A young girlfriend of Beth's told me at her funeral, "If I die, I wouldn't want my parents to be sad." It helped me appreciate that Beth and JonBenét would not want their dad in sorrow and mourning for the rest of his life.

Most of us live as if we have an unlimited number of days ahead of us, and we'll just go on forever. We tend to think we'll always have the same good people around us, parents, siblings, kids, friends, extended families—and it can cause us to be careless with our time and with those things that are really important, such as relationships and our faith walk with God. I've learned to do a better job of living for the day at hand, acknowledging each day as a gift. I read about a man who erected a tombstone for himself that had his name on it, the date he was born, but the date of his death was, of course, blank. Each morning he would go by the cemetery to remind himself that life is limited and this day was precious. A little bizarre, yes, but I guess it helped this man focus on his blessings and the present.

Beth would be in her forties now, and JonBenét would be graduating from college this year. My other children have families of their own. I am pleased that they take extraordinary time with their children. Time with the ones we love is perhaps one of life's greatest gifts.

Time. How easy to take it for granted. For us men, most of our time is spent around our work. Patsy understood the hours my job demanded and was gracious and accepting about the time I spent traveling and at work, but I think now about the kids.

They grew up so fast!

Today I no longer experience the joy of a child's "Daddy's home! Daddy's home!" when I walk in the door in the evening, and here I am, with all the time in the world to play ball, read stories—ride a bike—

"Daddy, pretty please, can we go around the block just one more time?"

"Not now, there's no time."

Thankfully, I can now hear the shouts of *"Grandpa's here!"*

The apostle Paul wrote, "...but one thing *I do*, forgetting those things which are behind and reaching forward to those things which are ahead" (Philippians 3:13).

Of course, we all have regrets, some more painful than others. Regret is natural, I suppose, if we let ourselves go there. It's an emotion like worry—it has no constructive value. It's taken me time and discipline to stop dwelling on my regrets. So many things I would change if I could, so many things I would do differently. I would fix the burglar alarm, I'd take that ride around the block—

I try to remember those words of the Apostle Paul. I speak them aloud. "I reach forward to those things which are ahead!"

I pray, *God, help me say good-bye to my regrets. Help me see that today is the first day of the rest of my life. Help me to see that I have a future that can be filled with hope.*

CHAPTER 15

The Power of Choice

*Finally, brethren, whatever things are true, whatever things are noble, whatever things are just,
whatever things are pure, whatever things are lovely,
whatever things are of good report, if there is any virtue and if
there is anything praiseworthy—meditate on these things.*

—Philippians 4:8

We face the storms of life with choices.

Vicktor Frankl, MD, PhD, was a Jewish physician and psychologist in Vienna in the 1930s, who was captured and imprisoned by the Nazis during World War II in the Auschwitz death camp. In his book, *Man's Search for Meaning*, he wrote:

We who lived in concentration camps can remember the men who walked through the huts comforting others, giving away their last piece of bread. They may have been few in number, but they offer sufficient proof that everything can be taken from a man but one thing: the last of the human freedoms—to choose one's attitude in any given set of circumstances, to choose one's own way.

Frankl's father died of starvation in the concentration camp. His wife, mother, and brother also died tortured deaths in the camps. Through it all, Frankl discovered that the meaning of life is found in every moment of living; and life never ceases to have meaning, even in suffering. After the loss of a loved one, we can live the remainder of our lives with regret, bitterness, and brokenness, or we can accept that we cannot change what has happened to us. We can make a conscious choice to go on with life, quite possibly a life with a deeper meaning and purpose because of our loss.

We alone have the authority and power to make that choice.

When all my children were with me, I thought I had life under control. My children were healthy, my home was a happy one, my business was doing well. I was gliding along through life in the "Lord giveth" lane.

It was quite a shock when I moved into the "Lord taketh" lane. When Beth died, I was not prepared spiritually. I had not built spiritual disciplines into my life, and I certainly didn't have an intimate relationship with God. In the Book of Job, it's obvious Job made a spiritual investment in his seventy years before tragedy struck because how else could he stay faithful to God in the midst of such devastation? Job obviously had been a spiritually disciplined man long before tragedy struck. He didn't just begin his prayer life that day. He already had a relationship with God.

Patsy was first diagnosed with Stage Four ovarian cancer in 1994. She was in remission for nine years and the cancer returned in 2002. Patsy didn't accuse God of failing her when the cancer returned. She didn't cry out "Why me?" She never once charged God for abandoning her. She didn't curse Him. She remained faithful.

The media painted us as rich, as being of an elite, privileged class, but we never considered ourselves elite or rich. I worked hard, was lucky to be in the right place at the right time, and after years of work, I had accumulated a respectable nest egg. Still, we didn't think of ourselves as rich. During one of the police interrogations, Patsy was asked, "Do you dress for dinner?" Patsy was startled by the question. "Do you mean, do we wear clothes?"

"No, like, do you guys get dressed up, you know, formal for dinner?"

Patsy held back a laugh. We ate most of our meals either at the kitchen counter or in the breakfast room, sitting with feet looped around the legs of the counter stools, unwrapping our take-out burgers and fries.

"Did anyone remember the catsup?"

"Uh-oh. I forgot. Maybe there's some in the fridge. Johnnie Bee, would you check the fridge and bring us the catsup?"

Much of the time we went to the restaurants the kids liked, especially Saturday mornings for waffles. Blueberry waffles with syrup and whipped cream. We ate in the dining room when we had company.

"We're an ordinary family," Patsy told the officer.

"Right. Ordinary." He scoffed.

But we *were* ordinary. One of the detectives doubted that Patsy would actually wear the same clothes two days in a row. He didn't think "rich people" did that. He considered her wearing the same clothes the morning of December twenty-sixth that she had worn the previous evening an indication of guilt. His conclusion was that she had never taken off her clothes that night to go to bed; after all, she had a closet full of clothes—why would she wear the same thing two days in a row?

Imagine a mom in a rush to get her family ready for their vacation trip, and she hurriedly throws on the clothes nearest her in the bathroom, still clean, a nice red sweater (red, for the holidays) and the slacks she wore only a couple hours—quickly, quickly; she has to get everyone up, prepare their breakfast, get the car packed, try not to forget anything—and be out the door on time.

I had a philosophy in business to never make a decision until I had to. It gave me time to get as much information as I could and therefore make the best decision possible, based on all the information at hand. I learned you can make big mistakes if you jump to conclusions or judge too quickly. It's dangerous to size up a situation in haste and by first impression draw conclusions. Such conclusions could bear absolutely no resemblance to the facts as they unfold. It's important, if time permits, to consider all facts, do the research, examine all sides, and remain open-minded. Professional detectives know this.

When we moved back to Atlanta after

JonBenét's death, we bought a three-bedroom, two-story brick house on Paces Ferry Road in a northwest suburb of Atlanta, and for safety purposes, installed security windows, state-of the-art burglar alarms, outdoor sensor lighting, iron gating in front, a high surrounding brick wall, double bolting locks—the place was like a fortress. We were still being stalked by the media, but we felt more secure being back in Atlanta, where we had been married, where our children were born, and where our extended family lived.

In this new house I had doors removed so there were only three entrances—front, back, and basement—unlike the six doors and more than thirty windows just on the main floor in our Boulder house. The windows in this new house were sealed shut and could not be opened. On the main floor we had reconfigured the rooms so that they flowed into each other through wide archways in order to have a totally open floor plan. Upstairs we made sure there was no hallway, only a small landing separating the three bedrooms.

I liked to do a lot of the work myself, and one day the Bulgarian workers I hired to do the heavy construction paid me a big compliment. The men saw me doing some interior painting one evening, and as I was cleaning up, the foreman said to me, "Hey dere! You vork hard yust like Bulgarian!" I took the comment as a terrific compliment. I had once been named "Businessman of the Year" for my accomplishments in business, but this statement by an earnest Bulgarian worker made me feel just as proud.

After the Bulgarians had completed their work on the house and we said *"Davizhdane,"* goodbye, I was alone in the house and preparing to put some shelves in a mudroom by the back door. I discovered I had run out of saw blades, so I hopped in my car to make a quick run to Home Depot. I didn't pause to set the alarm or lock the entrance gates, but I made sure to lock all the doors, and drove out the driveway and onto Paces Ferry to head for Home Depot. It would take me thirty minutes, tops.

When I came back, I saw a car in the driveway that was backed in with the front of the car facing the road. That seemed strange but I figured it was one of the Bulgarian men, or possibly the contractor. I entered the house through the garage door to look for the driver, but there was nobody around. I went into the foyer and a strange guy was coming down the front stairway carrying two suitcases. They happened to be my suitcases.

"Hey, who are you?"

"Uh, I'm a contractor."

"You're a contractor? I've never seen you before. And what are you doing with my suitcases?"

"These are my tools."

"I don't think so. I'm calling the police."

As soon as I said those words, he took a flying leap down the stairs and jumped me, throwing me to the floor. We fought for what seemed like an hour and I was mostly trying to get away from him, not subdue him.

"Where's the jewelry?" he demanded.

"What jewelry?"

"Your wife's jewelry."

"We don't believe in jewelry," I gasped. "It attracts thieves!"

I almost laughed at my little jab of humor, but then I thought maybe I should just cool it as this situation could turn really ugly. I could, I could—what? Reason with this guy?

"Listen," I wheezed, "I'll back off and you get out of my house, okay? Just *go*." The thought occurred to me that he could have a gun, or a knife, and this could turn out a whole lot worse.

"Yeah? You'll call the cops."

"Of course I'll call the cops. What do you think?"

More yanking, shoving, punching, and he jerked me into the bathroom and slammed me against the wall. Shaking to clear my head and getting to my feet, I heard him pushing our grandfather clock in front of the door. I decided maybe it was safe to be locked in the bathroom for the moment.

"Just get out of my house. *Now!*" I yelled. At that moment I noticed one of my large wood drill bits lying on the bathroom sink. I had a weapon! —No, leave it be, just get this guy out of the house. Common sense prevailed: The stuff in the suitcases is just stuff. I set the drill bit down.

The thief took off with his loot, including my laptop, Beth's college ring, my credit cards, my wallet, my driver's license—all packed in my good suitcases. The only item that really distressed me to lose was Beth's ring. She had been given it by her sorority as an honor for being an outstanding senior. I called the Atlanta police, and to my relief, they showed up within minutes, and not surprisingly, with them came the television helicopters hovering overhead.

Once again, we were news.

During all this, Patsy had been out with a friend from church having coffee when she saw on the news on the coffee shop TV that "the home of slain child, JonBenét Ramsey, was robbed this morning..."

She shot straight up out of her chair, nearly knocking over the table. "We were robbed? What?"

Meanwhile I was being transported to the hospital for my injuries, the worst of which was a partially detached retina. The surgery cost me $10,000. (No insurance. Patsy had cancer, and I was unemployed.)

The robber had gotten into our home by breaking down the one door in the basement. (I hadn't set the burglar alarm.) About a month later when I was recovering from my eye surgery the police asked me to come and look at a photo lineup. I pointed one guy out after studying the photos for several minutes. The officer said, "Are you one hundred percent positive that's the guy?"

"Well, I'm seventy percent sure."

"You must be one hundred percent positive. This is the one we've focused on as the guy who broke into your house. He usually strikes the homes where construction work is being done. The house he robbed before yours? He tied up the old couple living there."

"Well, I'm seventy percent sure this is the guy."

"But we need one hundred percent."

I couldn't say with 100 percent certainty that this was the guy.

We never retrieved Beth's ring or my laptop. The credit cards I replaced. I figured if they ever caught the guy, his punishment should be to go to the DMV for a replacement driver's license as I had to do. That's real punishment.

Once again the sanctity of our home was violated.

We lived a semisequestered life in that Atlanta house from 1997 to 2001, with regular visits to our cottage in Charlevoix during the summers. Burke attended the Lovett School in Atlanta for the middle grades and part of high school, and had completed his sophomore year when we made a family decision to move to Charlevoix, so he could finish high school in a small-town atmosphere. He was happy about the decision, and so were we. We hoped the media was tired of us by now, and prayed for a reprieve from their omnipresent glaring eye.

I had baffling recurring nightmares of being back in school and the math teacher is giving us an exam. I've missed classes, haven't studied, and don't have the textbook. The Bible is full of accounts of visions and dreams coming to God's people. Most of my life I didn't pay that much attention to my dreams, but I've learned that dreams are metaphors and can be messages from God. The dream of being unprepared for a test is exactly what happened to me. The dream was a picture of my spiritual life. I had not been prepared to handle the tests of life and I needed to get spiritual discipline in my life. There was so much I didn't know about the Lord, and this dream was a strong call to study the word of God, to pray and get spiritually fortified. With spiritual disciplines in my life, and the realization I have the right to choose my response to difficulty, I can be prepared to face life's challenges head-on.

CHAPTER 16

Resilience of the Spirit

*Outwardly we are wasting away,
yet inwardly we are being renewed day by day.
For our light and momentary troubles are achieving for us,
an eternal glory that far outweighs them all. So we fix our eyes
not on what is seen but on what is unseen.
What is seen is temporary,
what is unseen is eternal. (NIV)*
—2 Corinthians 4:16–18

People ask me if, after a certain length of time of trials, does a person develop emotional calluses so the sting doesn't go so deep? They want to know if a person's heart can harden with time; will the loss fade into the background, will insults, accusations, threats, and lies one day fall on deaf ears? Is it possible to develop psychological barriers so nothing gets through to hurt us anymore? My answer? Yes, but not for the reasons these people suggest. Suffering does have a beginning and an end. Given enough time, we humans have the unique ability to remember the good things of our past and render the bad memories to the background. "Memories that today bring pain will tomorrow bring smiles," was an admonition my minister, Dr. Harrington, gave me years ago and I found it to be very true.

When I think of Beth or JonBenét today, I think of them smiling and happy, and am grateful for the time each of them was in my life. I can endure the pain of losing them because it was so wonderful to have them, even for a short time.

We have an amazing capacity for resilience. History is full of examples of the resilience of the human spirit: Anne Frank, Helen Keller, and Nelson Mandela, just to name a few. The mindless accusations and lies that were told about my family came from a small minority. That minority had a loud voice in the form of the media, but that hurtful minority was countered by the kindness and compassion we felt from the people who supported and encouraged us. As corny as it sounds, I believe in the end that truth and justice do prevail finally. God despises injustice and will make things right, even if it takes a while.

We cannot let a crisis or tragedy determine our future. It's how we handle these things that determines our future. As my faith matured, I began to understand that God expects us, above all else, to trust Him. For someone like me who has trusted *myself* all my life, trusting God gave me a level of peace I had never experienced.

Patsy and I appeared on *Larry King Live* on March 27, 2000. It can be intimidating to sit on the set of a television show with a famous host, but we both preferred live broadcasts such as King's show. If the program was live, our comments couldn't be edited. At one point Larry King asked Patsy, "Do you believe your daughter is happier in Heaven right now?"

PATSY: I would like to think JonBenét would be happier here in my arms.

KING: Here's some of the things the police are saying that was supposed to have happened that didn't: you insisted the interviews be done together, you insisted that they be done in your lawyer's office, that Patsy Ramsey's doctor be present, that the Ramsey attorneys specifies which officer conducts the interview; that you seem to get special treatment; you were given a copy of the ransom note; transcripts of your initial talk with police officers; you were given initial police reports; you were given a list of questions you were going to be asked.

PATSY: Excuse me?

KING: Okay, is any of this true?

PATSY: The ransom note was in my home.

KING: They meant as evidence.

PATSY: We turned the ransom note over to them. We didn't demand a copy of the ransom note.

KING: This appears like—in other words, are these statements true?

JOHN: Well, look, I don't remember totally what is true and isn't true, but this is pettiness.

KING: No, if you say, I will only be interviewed together, we'll only be interviewed with our lawyer, they will only be interviewed in our office with our doctor, you're setting conditions that the average suspect can't set.

JOHN: Look, we didn't set any conditions.

KING: No? Okay.

JOHN: Our attorneys represented us. They were highly suspicious of the police and for good reason. The police were out to get us. We threw ourselves to the lions anyway. A good defense attorney will tell you that if they think the police are after their client, they shut up. They don't talk. They tell the police, go ahead and prove it. We insisted that we talk to the police. We came back to Boulder after we buried JonBenét for the primary reason to work with the police. We had no interest in going back to Boulder. Atlanta was our home. That's where we lived for twenty-five years before we moved to Colorado.

PATSY: I was afraid to go back to Boulder.

JOHN: We were afraid. We went back to work with the police to find the killer of our daughter. Our attorney sat us down and said, look, you need to understand something. First of all, your child's body was ransomed twice last week, once by the killer and once by the police. You need to understand who you're working with here. These people are not objectively looking for the killer. They are intent on convicting you of her death.

PATSY: So what are you going to do?

JOHN: We had to listen to them.

PATSY: You have to take the advice of your attorneys when they tell you something like that... We have to know and believe in our faith that we will see JonBenét again. She is in Heaven with our Heavenly father and one of these days, John and me—we will be there. We will be there with her, and we live for that day. That's what keeps us going.

JOHN: What it causes you to do, Larry, is to think what in the world is the purpose of life? Life's tough.

KING: Have the answer?

PATSY: It's real tough.

JOHN: I think the purpose in life is to prepare us for eternity.

And I meant it.

April 2006: We're on an airplane to Hawaii on our way to speak at the Easter services at Hope Christian Fellowship Church in Honolulu. Patsy is battling the last days of her cancer. The flight attendant wheels the beverage cart down the aisle and pauses at our seats. "Something to drink?" She doesn't recognize us. Patsy sits leaning forward in her seat. I order cranberry juice for both of us. Patsy tries to appear normal; she lifts her head and smiles a faint smile at the flight attendant, who hands her the plastic glass. Patsy's hand shakes as she reaches for the glass. I know I shouldn't lift my hand and do it for her. Just like I shouldn't help her with things she insists on doing herself: working a zipper, carrying her purse. This morning, back in Atlanta, getting dressed, she couldn't reach her feet to pull on her shoes. She sat slumped at the edge of the bed, her new beige shoe with the strap across the instep in her hand.

"Honey?"

"Yes, sweetheart, let me get that for you."

I joked with her about buying complicated

footwear. Her condition was going downhill, I knew that. No, I knew it and I didn't know it. She was still here, she was still Patsy, my Patsy, and we were still together. I had believed we would beat this cancer. We were going to go on with our lives together. We would travel to Hawaii to give our testimony and be an enccuragement to people.

"John, isn't it wonderful these Christians want us to come and speak? See? There are those who believe in us."

"Yes, Patsy, it's wonderful."

I touch the softness of her arm. I try to breathe deeply. Patsy, we have a life together, you and I. A future. We're above the world in this airplane and we're flying to Hawaii. Let's think of this trip as a second honeymoon. Let's thank God for this experience. The lights in the cabin dim for the in-flight movie to begin. A murder mystery. Not something we'd put earphones on to watch. We lean back in our seats hoping for sleep, but as I allow the monotonous sound of the cabin to overtake me, I can hear Patsy's labored breathing. I know and I don't know. I turn to see her face, her eyes pressed tight, mouth and jaw set in pain.

My hand moves for her face to gently touch her cheek. Her eyelids relax, her shoulders soften. The painkillers have kicked in and my fingers reach the smoothness of her skin as she drifts off. My index finger wipes away a bead of sweat, or is it a tear?

We are scheduled to speak at two services that will see ten thousand people come to celebrate Jesus' resurrection. At the entrance to the large tent set up especially for the services, Patsy holds on to my arm for balance. "John, do you think there are people here who still believe the lies of the media? Are there people in this church who still believe we killed our little girl?"

"I don't know. Probably. Well, yes." I was aware that there are a few who opposed our speaking at this church, those who still considered us *guilty as charged by the media* in spite of the overwhelming evidence of our innocence. (The final DNA analysis, which resulted in our official clearance, would not be released until 2008.) We understood the power of the media over public thought and opinion only too well. You publish a lie enough times and people will believe it's true. I knew there were those people who didn't think we deserved to stand at a church podium, who didn't want us darkening the doorway of their church.

"John, we can do this," Patsy said. "Hurting people need to know if we can make it, they can, too. You look good in a Hawaiian shirt. Be sure and smile."

Clasping hands, we prayed, "Thank You, Lord,

thank You for this Easter Sunday, please make our words Your words."

She had two months to live.

Easter Sunday in Oahu, and Patsy manages to sit near the front of the platform for the services. She squeezes my hand in encouragement as I'm introduced. She wears her blue silk suit and the drop pearl earrings I bought for her on vacation in Florida. She's too weak to walk to the platform and join me at the podium, but her nearness gives me confidence.

"My only credential to stand here before you this morning," I tell the congregation, "is that I am a fellow sufferer."

I tell the people that faith changes after tragedy. "Most of the time tragedy changes how one views God," I tell them. "Patsy and I had to learn to trust God in the deepest sense through tragedy and sorrow."

I look down to meet Patsy's eyes, she smiles at me, and I'm strengthened. I tell the audience about the challenge my friend posed to me several years before: "John, you must get to a place where you believe the best days of your life are still in front of you. That is hope and we all must have hope in our lives."

I tell them God keeps His promises to us.

I finish my message and am surprised as the

crowd rises to their feet applauding. I am humbled because I wasn't sure my message was good enough. Patsy is standing, too. Later I would drive her to the Honolulu hospital for a blood transfusion.

Two months.

The next day we appeared on the TV program *Connecting Point* with Pastor Wayne Cordeiro. He was kind in the interview but asked difficult questions such as, would we support the death penalty for the killer of our baby?

"No!" Patsy responded without hesitating. "Killing another person is stooping to the same level as the murderer."

She went on to tell the television audience, "I pray for this person who killed my child. I pray for his salvation. I believe God is a God of justice." I watched her pretty face now swollen from the medication, her charming smile still warm and friendly. She was passionate about trusting God. "Even if JonBenét's murderer is never caught in my lifetime," she told Pastor Cordeiro, "I have peace in the fact that God will take care of it. He is the ultimate judge."

We sat on the sofa of the set with fresh orchid leis around our necks, the Hawaiian symbol of welcome, as Patsy struggled with the nausea and pain of the growing cancer. She had forgiven the killer, she said. I listened to her with pride. I was still struggling with forgiveness. At that point, I believed in the case of murder, forgiveness could only be granted by God or the victim. I could forgive this creature for ruining our lives and destroying our family, but the ultimate forgiveness for murder was the right of the ultimate victim, JonBenét. For a long time I thought quick death was too lenient a punishment for such a vile creature as this person who killed our daughter.

In all our interviews I found that I was calm and eager to answer any question posed. It didn't seem to matter that millions of people could be watching and listening. I told Pastor Cordeiro that there was a time when I personally would have welcomed death because my grief was so great.

"I realized," I said, "that if death is a relief, then death can't really be the ultimate penalty." I could forgive the Boulder police for their carelessness, and people of the news media for their cruelty, but the killer? I wasn't there yet.

The TV interview concluded, and in spite of her weakness, Patsy stepped down to talk with people in the audience. She stood and chatted for nearly an hour, and then I took her arm and guided her outside, where our rental car waited. She fell limp into the seat. "John, weren't these people wonderful?" The sky was a brilliant cobalt blue, the sun bright; it was the kind of day a married couple like us should head for the beach together, lie in the sun, walk barefoot on the white sand, have lunch under the palms, but these were leisure activities for other people, not us.

Only two months.

It would be a long, hard flight home, but we hoped our testimonies in Hawaii had helped someone. We wanted the lessons of our moving to the other side of suffering to help others.

The mind at peace, the body in turmoil.

Patsy rarely slept longer than an hour or two at a time before she needed more pain medication. Would God heal her again? Back in Atlanta, we moved into her dad's single-level home. Patsy could no longer climb stairs.

Two months became one month.

One month.

Thirty days.

Patsy beckoned to me from the bed, where she was reading our mail, to share a letter from a woman in Canada. "This woman is saying how touched she was by JonBenét's story. Listen to this: 'JonBenét has affected the lives of many more people in her short six years than many of us strive for in a lifetime.'"

Patsy's face softened in smiles. "Oh, John, I would sure like to think that's true. Our little Johnnie Bee, we knew she would be very special in this world, didn't we?" She paused. "But not like this."

"Patsy, she is special. This letter illustrates that we probably don't know the half of it."

"Yes, honey—but do you think she accomplished her purpose in this life in her six short years?"

"I don't think I can answer that for sure."

She was quiet for a moment, then said in a positive voice, "John, I'm not afraid to join her. I'm so looking forward to seeing her."

"I know. But I want you here."

She took my hand, stroked the palm. "John, we're going to have to find you another wife."

"No! Thanks, but I'm happy with the wife I've got!"

"Well, I'm just saying..."

"Don't."

Every day we prayed for a miracle. Every day her condition grew worse.

CHAPTER 17

Saying Good-bye

The light of faith makes us see what we believe.
—Thomas Aquinas

The day Patsy died seemed like just days after the death of our little girl, though it had been ten years. I wanted her to stay, not to leave me. Facing life alone without Patsy was almost unimaginable. Two weeks earlier, her doctor took my arm, sat me down. It was midmorning and the sun had just invaded the room through the cracks in the window blinds. The humidity and heat steamed the lawn and the walkway outside.

"John, it's time we consider palliative care... hospice."

Hospice.

"We'll make her as comfortable as possible. I'm so sorry. More chemotherapy and radiation treatments would just be torture without any benefit."

She couldn't handle more treatments, more chemotherapy. It was over.

Until this last occurrence I wouldn't accept she was going to die. From the beginning, I believed we were going to beat this thing. With Beth and JonBenét's deaths there was nothing I could do to make the outcome different; I couldn't get them to the best hospitals, I couldn't bring in the best doctors with the latest technology, but with Patsy I could do something to change the outcome. With prayer and the latest medical care, we would beat this and she would make it. When the cancer moved to her brain, we still kept fighting. Go for the gamma knife surgery, the major procedures, anything to beat this monster—I kept thinking we're going to lick this—even though, I confess, deep down I recognized with each recurrence, the battle was getting more difficult. In this last battle our weapons were of no use. The chemotherapy and radiation treatments were having no effect, and her condition deteriorated fast. Now she was in agonizing pain and no longer able to comprehend what was going on around her.

The most difficult decision of my life was when

I decided to follow her doctor's recommendation and stop the chemotherapy and radiation treatments. I was throwing in the towel and preparing Patsy's death certificate, I knew that. We both had fought this cancer for twelve years. We had won many battles but we were going to lose the war. I couldn't bring myself to tell her there would be no more chemotherapy or radiation treatments. Now we were going to do everything we could to make her last days comfortable and full of love. It broke my heart to think that Burke would lose his mother. He was too young. She had been in remission for nine years, and now my gentle Patsy lay a ghostly shell laboring for each breath. All we could do was pray for God to take her home; God, no more suffering.

Once we had a life, a good life, Patsy and I. We were supposed to grow old together. I expected to be the first to leave, as I was thirteen years older than Patsy. All of our financial planning anticipated that happening. Now the threat of death was very real and very near, but it was Patsy who was leaving, not me.

She had been my strong supporter in everything I tried to accomplish. Through her years of suffering with ovarian cancer, she was full of hope. She was the most optimistic person I have ever known. She had ironclad faith in God, despite the fact that

He allowed the poison of cancer to run rampant in her body.

Patsy, my vivacious, fun-loving, talented wife, now withered and bald... dying.

The hospice nurses told me it was important that I release Patsy from this earth and give her permission to go. Otherwise, she would quite possibly hang on, for me and her family.

Approaching her comatose body, I whispered in her ear, "I love you, Patsy. But Patsy, I have to let you go... it's okay, you can go home. Burke and I will be all right."

The day Patsy died did not begin like any other day. This was the day that came to us as an intrusion, an unwelcome visitor with heavy luggage. Yet we had known for a long time that this visitor was coming. It signaled the end of a beautiful life. Patsy and I were married when she was twenty-three years old and she dedicated her whole life to me and our family. I can only hope I gave her a life good enough to merit that commitment. This good-bye would be final—

No, I remind myself, it is not final. I'll see her again.

That early morning in June as I lay beside her

in bed with her breathing unsteady, each breath a struggle, I felt the memories of our twenty-five years of marriage fill my thoughts. *Oh, Patsy, you're leaving me. You're leaving me.*

Death clouded my world once again; the sharp, jagged pains were about to resume. Patsy's hand in mine, still wearing her wedding ring, my bride. I dabbed her mouth with the lip swab, and told her once again, "I love you. It's okay to go." I stroked her cheek, her forehead. Her heart rate quickened rapidly. The oral medicine I gave her had no effect. I knew this was the end. Then suddenly, and just for a moment, her eyes opened wide as if surprised, as if seeing something wondrous beyond me, beyond the room. And with one final release of breath, she stepped into the arms of Jesus.

Outside, dawn was still hours away. The thick Georgia humidity forewarned of the June heat and made tears come more easily. The dew was eager for the earth, and Heaven was eager for my wife. The silence—silence loud, bewildering, a world put on pause.

With Patsy still in my arms, my teenage son asleep at the other end of the house, and an early morning sun about to rise, I could do nothing but lie there. Then up they came, the sobs, admitting the end, an avalanche of sobs from the heart, as though all the sobs of every husband left behind heaved forth out of me.

There's an earsplitting quietness of death. The vivid memory of the last breath, and then the absence. My wife, still warm, in my arms.

Oh, Patsy. Patsy.

Burke. I had to tell Burke. How do I tell my son his mother is dead? Do I say Mom's in Heaven, son? Do I just say she's gone? No matter how I say it, the words are terrible. We had held on day by day praying for a miracle, pretending that this day would never come. Burke had been strong throughout it all, but I am sure he knew this moment was coming.

"Burke," I whispered. He turned his head to me, his eyes squinting in the shard of light from the hallway. "Burke..."

"What, Dad?"

"Burke..."

"What's wrong?"

"I'm sorry, son..."

"It's Mom, isn't it?"

"Yes, I'm sorry, son..."

Neither of us could speak. I reached for him, and for a moment we held each other without words and cried. His mother was dead, and his world was forever changed.

Balloons. Patsy wanted balloons. "John, listen to me. I want a party when I go home," she had insisted. "I'll be celebrating in Heaven and I want you all to celebrate with me. Will you do that for me?"

She wanted balloons. Patsy wanted balloons.

"Balloons at a funeral, Patsy?" I had asked her. "Yes, balloons," she said, her voice resolute. "I want my funeral to be a celebration. I'll have graduated to Heaven. Isn't that something to celebrate?"

"Oh, Patsy..."

"And hats! I want the women to wear big, fancy hats, like at a fabulous garden party. I want a party atmosphere. No tears. No sadness."

When you live with cancer for so many years of your life, you learn to coexist with the threat of death always looming around the corner, and in the spaces between pleasant moments. You never know when it will make its call, what day, what hour, what year. Oh God, we had prayed, give her another year. Another year.

But now it was final. There would be no more dreading the day, anticipating the worst. The day was here.

We had balloons and her lady friends wore hats just as she wanted, but I couldn't follow her directions on one detail. She had said no tears. There were plenty of tears. Despite the beautiful music, the lovely service, and the hundreds of loving people, there were tears.

Patsy, the life of the party, was not there. Patsy, greatly loved and cherished by so many people for her generous spirit, her compassionate and happy heart, her kindness and fun-loving personality, was not there to cheer us up, organize things, and keep everyone happy. There were too many people to shake all their hands. The service was held at the Roswell United Methodist Church, outside Atlanta. I remember only some of the words of the minister: "Patsy is in a place where there's no more suffering, no more pain..." *Oh God, help me.*

I couldn't imagine how it was going to be possible to get from the church to the Saint James Episcopal Cemetery, which was twenty miles away and through some of Atlanta's most notorious traffic. As we left the church and progressed down the busy streets, I looked out the window of the car and saw one of the most touching sights of all my life: Policemen in full uniform stood at attention with their hats off as we approached each intersection, having stopped traffic for our procession. I also saw workers stop their labor, take off their hard hats, and hold them to their chests as we passed. I was moved to tears at this courtesy—

it felt as though they were saying *We know what you've been through. We're standing with you. Rest in peace.*

The media showed up, of course; there they were with their cameras and their recorders and their notepads, but they were courteous this time. I had buried two children and now I was burying my wife, their graves next to each other in the cemetery: Elizabeth Pasch Ramsey, JonBenét Patricia Ramsey, and now Patricia Paugh Ramsey. When the burial service ended, hundreds of colored balloons were released into the sky. Yes, Patsy, we celebrated your graduation.

One night after Patsy's funeral I sat alone in my room feeling there was no place on earth I could go to start over, when Burke came into the room and sat down beside me. He had been very close to his mom, and Patsy adored him. Here was a boy entering manhood full of promise. I looked at his young face and resolved then and there to join the living and continue to do the best I could to make a decent life for this young man who deserved better than a self-pitying dad. Burke's pain was no less than mine.

I had to be both mother and father now. Patsy was so involved with his life, the loving, doting mom, and now I had to pick up where she had left off. When JonBenét was born, I was in my forties and I prayed to live to be at least seventy-five so she would be a grown woman before she lost her father. Now I realized my boy needed a dad who wasn't an old, defeated shadow of a human being, but a real live, loving, strong dad.

Patsy had been cancer-free for two years before JonBenét's death, and she remained cancer-free until 2002. She fought against the disease until it finally took her. She knew the remission had been a gift from God so she could enjoy her family and give us and life all she had.

And I was grateful. Oh, I was grateful.

Patsy's death was forewarned and didn't strike suddenly and tragically as it did with Beth and JonBenét, so the aftermath of her home-going presented a different kind of emotional trauma. I've talked to men and women who've lost their partners to long-term diseases, and they've said that after years of caring for their loved one, agonizing with their suffering, loving them and praying for them, begging God for more time, they actually felt a sense of peace at their death. It's inexplicable, really, that feeling. Perhaps it's because you don't want them to suffer any longer.

It's a blessing to know when our loved ones leave us, they're with God in Heaven. This confidence is a gift of faith.

Yes, Patsy is with God, thank you, Jesus, but I'm

still here. And "here" is both an end and a beginning.

During my suffering after JonBenét's death, I moved very close to God. When I opened myself up to His holy, loving embrace, something happened inside me that was wonderful. I so much wanted to be more receptive to God's love and guidance that I began to spend more time listening for the voice of God. I would imagine that I was sitting by a small stream talking to Jesus, who was sitting next to me. I would try and quiet my mind and then talk and listen for as long as I could maintain that image of Him beside me in my mind.

"Abide in Me, and I in you. As the branch cannot bear fruit of itself, unless it abides in the vine, so neither can you, unless you abide in Me..."

I was climbing hand-over-foot to the other side of suffering.

I found myself more alone than I ever had been in my life. Jesus made companions out of solitude and silence. He withdrew often into solitude to hear from, and be strengthened by, His Heavenly father. I had to learn the difference between solitude and loneliness. When I'm alone with God, I can't be lonely. In the hours I withdraw to be alone with Him, I learn much about Him, but also a lot about myself.

I've never liked being alone. A bustling family,

social activities, hard work, and good friends have always been important to me. My twenty-five years married to Patsy were filled with all of these things. Patsy loved people in general. She loved entertaining, loved being involved in the children's school activities, as well as community affairs. We had a rich and fulfilling social life, and now I was without her, without my business, without a social calendar, and with an empty nest.

Often, before spending time with God, I'd take a deep breath and open the Bible, turning to the words of Jesus: *Peace I give you...* I spoke these words out loud to myself. *Peace He gives to me...* and slowly, slowly my mind would begin to clear of its clutter. I'd read the Beatitudes, *Blessed are the poor in spirit, For theirs is the Kingdom of Heaven...,* trying to get my thoughts on Him, not on me or my problems. Often, I would just go to the Psalms and start reading from the first one I turned to.

The word *hope* for some time remained a foreign concept for me. After the loss of my two daughters and living "under the umbrella of suspicion" for so many years, hope did not feel like a ready option available to me. But, oh, how I needed hope. Especially now.

CHAPTER 18

The Greatest of Christian Promises

Your kingdom is *an everlasting kingdom,*
And Your dominion endures *throughout all generations.*
—Psalm 145:13

Patsy was gone.

Well-meaning people will tell you that your loved one is happier now, they're with God. Isn't that wonderful? Shouldn't we be grateful?

I nod my head.

Yes, yes, that's true. Yes...

People feel compelled to say something helpful or encouraging to someone grieving, and that's very thoughtful, but I've found the most important thing someone can do is just be there. It's not necessary to say anything profound or meaningful. A simple, extended hug speaks volumes and sometimes is all that is necessary. Just being present helps immensely.

C. S. Lewis put it well in his book *A Grief Observed* (HarperCollins, 1994). He said after the loss of his wife, "I want others to be about me. I dread the moments when the house is empty. If only they would talk to one another and not to me."

Patsy and I were blessed to have good friends who surrounded us when we lost Beth and JonBenét. Friends were in the room; they were around us in person. They were *there*. It was immensely comforting just to see a friend nearby, crying with me, bringing me food, talking or not talking.

In grief, it is not uncommon to question God and His sovereign ways. How do you rationalize a loving God when in the depths of suffering? When C. S. Lewis lost his wife to cancer after only three short years of life together, he accused God of handing out happiness only to snatch it away. Grief is grief no matter how smart we are, no matter how venerated, rich or poor. His beloved wife died an anguished death, same as my Patsy.

I've been asked if the death of Beth prepared me for the death of JonBenét, and if JonBenét's death prepared me for the death of Patsy. The answer is yes, because my faith and beliefs were challenged and then strengthened because of those challenges.

When Beth died, I had a very shallow understanding of God and what He promised us as His children. I wasn't sure if I really bought into the Jesus story. I called myself a Christian without understanding really what I believed, so Beth's death caused me to question and examine my faith for the first time in earnest. I wanted to know if there really was eternal life and if I would see her again. It became critically important for me to get a clear understanding about the afterlife.

"For God so loved the world that He gave His only begotten Son, that whoever believes in Him should not perish but have everlasting life," Jesus said in John 3:16. Was this greatest of Christian promises true? I began to study, listen, and learn. Through a driving intellectual curiosity, I came to believe in my mind what the Bible says is true. That belief moved from an acceptance in my mind to a faith in my heart. The intellectual part of me was satisfied, and my heart was opened.

When JonBenét died, I had no doubt that she was in Heaven with God. My deep agony was for *my* loss, not JonBenét's. I had lost part of my future here on earth. Thankfully my spiritual journey continued and I recognized that this journey would be a lifelong event. I needed to continue to invest in it through study, prayer, and quiet time with God.

One of my spiritual mentors, a man who taught me how to study the Bible after Beth's death, told me, "John, I believe that JonBenét and Beth did not spend one more day or one less day on this earth than God intended for their lives." That thought was difficult for me to accept and understand. It illustrates the apparent conflict between man's free will and the sovereignty of God.

I believe that God gave man free will so that man could choose to love Him, much as I chose to love my wife. Without that free will component to man, we would just be God's robots. Yet I have to acknowledge that God is sovereign and all-powerful. I believe man's free will gone wrong resulted in JonBenét's murder. But was it God's sovereignty that allowed such a terrible thing to happen?

I had accepted that Jesus was exactly who he said he was. God, who came to earth in the form of man to both teach us and provide a sacrifice for a God of perfect justice. I began to think of myself as a follower of Jesus, not an Episcopalian or a Presbyterian. It made things so simple and clear. Jesus didn't come to earth only to be a sacrifice for our sins; He also instructed us to be His disciples, and to make other disciples. In other words, to follow Him, learn from Him, be like Him, and help other men and women do the same. Pretty clear and simple, but also a calling that takes a lifetime to absorb and do.

I will never be able to comprehend the full significance of human suffering nor this conflict between man's free will and God's sovereignty. Job realized the futility of questioning God about his troubles. We can question, argue, and be angry with Him, and He calmly responds as He did to Job, *"Where were you when I laid the foundations of the Earth? Tell* Me, *if you have understanding."*

God was saying to me through His Word, *"John, be quiet and listen to Me. I can see the whole picture. You cannot."*

I must accept that He works all things together for good, even though I don't understand the reasons or purpose of suffering. I must remind myself I don't have the eternal picture. I can only see what is before my eyes. I don't have vision for the unseen.

Job reached peace at last. "But now my eye sees You," he declared in Job 42:5, and what beautiful five simple words those are.

Now my eye sees You.

A lingering cloud of suspicion still loomed over my head. It was no longer black and ominous, but it was still there. It will always be there to some degree, I suspect. Once a reputation is tarnished, it never can be restored to pure white, even if the reputation was tarnished unjustly.

A number of years ago a high government official emerged from a Senate hearing which had just cleared him of wrongdoing, and he remarked to the waiting media, "Now would someone please tell me where I can go to recover my good reputation?" The point was, there was nowhere he could go. Patsy was gone, and it became important for me to try to restore her good name. I was no longer employed by Access Graphics after General Electric took over, and I was finding it almost impossible to regain a foothold in the business world.

One company president told me, "John, we would love to have you working for us, but we can't afford the risk of having our company's good name appear on the front page of the *National Enquirer*." That was the baggage I was stuck with.

I was pleased when a respected nationally broadcast Christian TV program invited me for an interview. I was anxious to share how the Lord was giving me hope in the face of my circumstances. Maybe by sharing my experiences, I could help others. I thought the interview went well, but I was stunned after the close when the interviewer asked me, "So, John—what do I tell my pastor friends when they ask me whether or not they should let you in their church?"

I paused. Let me in their church? *Should they let me in their church?* I wouldn't have expected that comment from a Christian. I lifted my eyes. His tone had changed, his stare was challenging, and he seemed proud of this hardball question. I said, "Well, if I'm a murderer, which apparently some people still think I am, it seems like I should be the first one they'd welcome into their church. What would you tell these pastors regarding Moses or King David? They were murderers. Would a church today refuse entry to two of the greatest heroes of the Bible and two of the most significant servants of God?"

He looked startled, then ashamed. "Yes, you're right." He then recounted an experience when he was young. He was refused entry to a cathedral in New York because he was dressed in rough motorcycle apparel.

"Jesus was not judgmental and we who make up God's church should not be either," I said, looking him squarely in the eye.

"Of course. Of course," he said.

CHAPTER 19

DNA Points JonBenét's Case in a New Direction

If you pray for bread and bring no basket to carry it, you prove the doubting spirit which may be the only hindrance to the gift you ask.
—D. L. Moody

July 10, 2008, at 12:05 a.m.
Headline: DISTRICT ATTORNEY SAYS TESTS SHOW UNIDENTIFIED MAN MURDERED CHILD

Twelve years after JonBenét Ramsey's murder, science took a leap that provided new hope of finding her killer and led authorities to exonerate her family.

On Wednesday, July 10, 2008, Boulder District Attorney Mary Lacy announced that a new method of collecting and analyzing DNA had generated new forensic evidence in JonBenét's case that led her to conclude that an unidentified man murdered our daughter, JonBenét, in our home on Christmas night in 1996.

The media release went on to explain that this new technique was able to extract minute DNA samples from other areas of JonBenét's clothing. The district attorney in her media release cleared Patsy, me, and the rest of my family of any involvement in JonBenét's murder. It stated:

"The Boulder District Attorney's Office does not consider any member of the Ramsey family, including John, Patsy or Burke Ramsey, as suspects in this case. We make this announcement now because we have recently obtained this new scientific evidence that adds significantly to the exculpatory value of the previous scientific evidence. We do so with full appreciation for the other evidence in this case."

The media release also included an apology, expressing deep regret for contributing in any way to the public perception that someone in the Ramsey family had committed the crime of murdering my daughter.

The statement read, "No innocent person should

have to endure such an extensive trial in the court of public opinion, especially when public officials have not had sufficient evidence to initiate a trial in a court of law."

Patsy and I had become the butt of late-night television jokes, glaring headlines, and talk show chatter. Patsy, who had been dead for two years now, became a particular target of media and Internet speculation and suspicion that created an "ongoing living hell for the Ramsey family and their friends," Lacy's statement said.

In 1997, DNA samples could only be recovered from relatively large deposits, such as blood or saliva. The new touch DNA process can recover DNA samples from minute deposits as small as a few skin cells. The Bode Technology Group, a forensic lab in Virginia, found unknown male skin cells on other areas of JonBenét's clothing, which, after analysis, matched the previously acquired genetic material recovered in blood found in JonBenét's underpants early in the investigation.

"DNA is very often the most reliable forensic evidence we can hope to find, and we rely on it often to bring to justice those who have committed crimes," it says in the statement.

I was grateful for the work Mary Lacy and her

staff continued to do and thankful for this new development. It brought us one step closer to finding JonBenét's killer. The untold story surrounding this event happened several years earlier when a friend asked me how he could pray for me. I told him we had been praying that God would cause the jurisdiction of JonBenét's case to be removed from the Boulder police and transferred to a more competent jurisdiction. I went on to tell him our prayers had not been answered so far. My friend thought a moment and then said, "John, you need to be more specific in your prayers. You need to ask God to raise someone up who has both the authority and the courage to move the jurisdiction. Yes, be more specific!"

I began to pray that God would raise up someone in authority who had the courage to do what would be very difficult and unusual to do: change the investigative agency responsible for JonBenét's murder investigation. A few months after beginning to pray that prayer, Mary Lacy removed the case from the police department and took control of the investigation. This DNA testing was a result of the work done by that new investigative team. Mary Lacy was the person God raised up to answer our prayer. Yes, she had some authority to do this but it took a tremendous level of courage to take over the investigation.

When I appeared on *The Oprah Show* a few months later, Oprah read the letter of clearance and apology to her audience. She asked if I forgave the media. I said yes. The DNA evidence had been there all along, but the police chose to first ignore it, then tried to explain it away. One veteran prosecutor said incredulously, "I have never in twenty years of prosecuting crimes ever seen a police department try and explain away foreign male DNA in a sexual assault case."

The media reported the news of the DNA test results and our clearance widely without spin or innuendo, even though it made their past reporting look flawed and reckless.

Oh, Patsy, our lawyers are saying the whole world owes us an apology. Isn't that something? I just wish this had happened while you were here.

CHAPTER 20

Forgiveness: A Gift to Ourselves

I can forgive but I cannot forget is only another way of saying, I cannot forgive.
—Henry Ward Beecher

Almost from the moment we realized JonBenét was murdered, I prayed to God to reveal the truth. Reveal who killed our daughter. At first my prayers were based on intense anger and a desire for revenge. The Bible tells us not to repay evil with evil. That was exactly what I had in mind. I knew if I found this faceless creature, I was very capable of tearing him limb from limb and I would have no remorse. For a long time, I told friends, you put me in a room with this monster and in sixty minutes there will be no need for a trial. I needed that much time to make sure he suffered before he died.

In time, I began to recognize that this rage, if acted upon, would make me no better a person than the man who murdered JonBenét. Repaying evil with evil wasn't right. As my rage quieted, the prayers to find the killer became a matter of proving our innocence. Then, after a long time, it became a matter of just wanting to know why? Why? Why? What did we do wrong?

An accused sex offender named John Mark Karr had implied in a long string of e-mail conversations with Dr. Michael Tracy, a University of Colorado journalism professor, that he had something to do with JonBenét's death. Karr was living in the heart of Bangkok, Thailand, and working as a teacher in a school for expatriate children. The cloak and dagger detective work to locate Karr involved the district attorney's investigators, Boulder County law enforcement agencies, Colorado State law enforcement, London Police, Roswell, Georgia, police, the Secret Service, Homeland Security, the Royal Canadian Mounted Police, and the Bangkok police. The work of these skilled law enforcement agencies renewed my confidence in law enforcement capabilities, and what they can accomplish when working together under strong leadership. Karr was arrested to face two-year-old charges of child pornography in California, which would give the authorities time to investigate him further. They needed his DNA, and if the DNA matched and he was in Boulder that night, he quite likely was the killer.

We had received many false confessions over the years. Most were obvious frauds. One confessor contacted our priest in Boulder and said he had killed JonBenét and wanted to turn himself in. Before he did, though, he wanted to talk to me. I talked with the man for forty-five minutes with a tape recorder running, and when he asked for money to buy airline tickets for himself and his wife to fly to Denver so he could turn himself in, a red flag went up. We notified the Boulder police of the caller but they were uninterested. The chief of police, Mark Beckner, said, "Well, if he wants to confess, tell him to come see us." Our own investigators eventually tracked the guy down to his home in Ohio and confronted him. He was a fraud, simply trying to extort money from me.

Karr was another imposter, but what I learned from the ordeal was that when the killer is eventually captured, I'd be faced with having to hear all the details of JonBenét's death. I wasn't sure I was prepared to hear what had happened to our child that night.

I had complained to a friend that God had not answered my constant prayer for the killer to be brought to light, and my friend wisely responded, "Perhaps God knows you are not ready for that day yet."

I understood what he meant. God knew I needed to be emotionally and spiritually prepared to handle the painful details of our child's death, and the inevitable grueling public trial. I had never read the autopsy report because I knew it would be too painful. I had never seen the photographs. Denial can be a powerful weapon to combat fear. Now with a trial, I would be forced to learn exactly what happened. This would be very, very difficult for me.

Despite the horror that I'm afraid my innocent baby experienced that night, I believe God was with her and was protecting her soul. I received some assurance of this two years after my daughter Beth was killed. A Delta flight attendant wrote me a letter and explained she was one of the first people to come up to the crumpled car in which Beth was riding. She told me that Beth's head was resting on her boyfriend's shoulder and she had the most peaceful look about her. I cried when I read the letter even though it gave me great comfort. When I found JonBenét that horrible morning, her delicate eyelids were closed and she looked very much at peace. While God didn't intervene in either of their deaths, I believe He was present with them, protecting them in a way I cannot begin to understand, and He welcomed their souls home with the unconditional love of a Father.

When Karr's DNA didn't match, he was released from custody within a few weeks of his arrest. California authorities had lost the evidence necessary to prosecute him for child pornography, so he was a free man, once again.

This episode also forced me to seriously examine the concept of forgiveness. Up to that point, I didn't have a name or a face to forgive, but for those few weeks I did have a face and a name of the possible killer. I wasn't sure how I felt. In the beginning, I would have torn this creature to pieces if I could have gotten my hands on him. Eventually, I decided that only JonBenét or God could forgive the murderer. I did not have the right to forgive him for taking JonBenét's life. "Forgiveness to the injured does belong" (John Dryden).

In 2003, a crazed milk truck driver walked into the West Nickel Mines Amish School armed with a 9mm semiautomatic pistol, bound ten little girls with wire and plastic restraints, stood them at the blackboard, and fired. He killed five of the children, critically wounding the others. These Amish families were faced with the most crushing blow evil can deliver, yet they did not respond with outrage, but instead said they had forgiven the gunman "through God's help." The world was impressed with this Christian spirit of forgiveness, but I wondered if they really did forgive deep down in their heart. How could they forgive such an inhuman planned attack on innocent children? I knew the rage I felt when JonBenét was murdered. These Amish parents knew something I didn't.

In the Greek New Testament, the word *apolusis* is used for forgiveness and it means to release. To forgive is to release the rage, the hurt, and the desire for revenge. Forgiveness is a gift I would give myself. Much like a ship at anchor being constantly battered by waves and wind, it will continue to be battered as long as it is anchored in place. Once the anchor is released and the ship is liberated of the anchor, it's free to sail on ahead, with purpose, free from the constant battering. Forgiveness had nothing to do with the one I was forgiving. It was a gift I could give myself. I could release the anchor to my soul and stop the battering. I could live again and move ahead.

CHAPTER 21

Are the Best Days Ahead?

*We also glory in tribulations,
knowing that tribulation produces perseverance;
and perseverance, character; and character,
hope.
Now hope does not disappoint.*
—Romans 5:3–5

I'm getting ready to go to dinner with friends. I shower, shave, stare at my clothes in the closet. The blue shirt; I'll wear the blue shirt. Beige pants. Beige socks. No need for a tie. I put on the blue shirt, the beige pants. I sit on the edge of the bed, pull on the beige socks, reach for the shoes. Shoes need polishing. I look at the floor, I'm deep in thought. Some things require deep thought.

Though I've turned down the sound, the murmur of the TV catches my attention. Someone else has been murdered. More young men are dead in Iraq. A storm brews over the Atlantic. In order to be happy we need designer faucets and a more robust beer. A bear and a moose bounce along a grassy knoll in the name of chocolate. Then back to war; a fire on the West Side; illegal aliens caught transporting dope; it looks like scattered rain tonight. I reach for the shoes.

Newscasts can be depressing. Someone has died on the freeway. Someone's been robbed. Someone's wounded, someone's missing. Every day more parents weep for their children. I feel my shoulders sag with the weight.

I heard a psychiatrist say once, "If you're depressed, turn off the television news."

I'm thinking about broken hearts. I understand that scientists have now discovered a *gene* that is linked to both physical and emotional pain. A gene. These genetic scientific findings indicate that a broken heart *really does* hurt, physically. I recently heard Dr. Francis Collins speak at the National Prayer Breakfast in Washington, D.C. Dr. Collins led the multiyear effort to document the complete human genome. It was a massive project, perhaps one of the greatest accomplishments of science to date. Dr. Collins explained that finding a single abnormal gene in a human being was like looking for a burned-out lightbulb that was in someone's basement, somewhere in America. The body continues to demonstrate to me the infinite complexity of God.

I rise to my feet; I pause at the mirror to whisk a brush through my hair. When JonBenét was murdered, our hearts were broken seemingly beyond repair. I can't forget how Patsy, drowning in grief, couldn't stand up, talk, or so much as hold a fork to eat. She had to be bathed, dressed, and fed. I would have chosen any torture on earth over that of losing my child. At the time, our hearts seemed broken beyond repair.

We were both suffering with chest pains. Patsy tried to explain the feeling of suffocating for lack of breath. Her doctor, a kind woman with burnt blond hair pulled back in a ponytail and wearing a herringbone suit, confirmed, yes, our hearts indeed were broken. She gave us the name for it. "It's called cardiomyopathy," she explained, "a temporary heart condition brought on by stressful situations, such as the death of a loved one."

"Many people who have broken heart syndrome may have severe chest pain or may think they're having a heart attack," the doctor said. "Your symptoms have been brought on by the heart's reaction to a huge surge of stress hormones, such as adrenaline. A part of your heart temporarily enlarges, and it could feel like you're having a heart attack."

"My heart *is* attacked," Patsy wailed.

"Will we ever feel better?" I wanted to know.

"Yes, Mr. Ramsey. Broken heart syndrome is treatable and patients usually recover."

At dinner, a friend asked me, "John, do you believe the best days of your life are ahead of you?" I must have given him a look that said, *Are you kidding?* By then I had lost two children, my employment, most of my life savings, my home, and my wife. The best days were ahead of me?

"No, that's impossible," I said. I wasn't being sarcastic, just honest.

"Well, John," he went on, "you need to get to a point where you believe the best days of your life are still ahead of you!"

It was a profound challenge and I knew he was right. I had been looking ahead, trying to survive, day to day, but really just kind of putting in my time until I died. I didn't know how to look forward with anticipation that the future would be better than ever. How could my best days still be in front of me?

One of the ways I learned to reestablish hope in my life was to find something to look forward to. I tell myself: In three weeks I'll see my son, John Andrew. In two months we'll all be together for Thanksgiving. Sometimes I make these looking forward times more immediate. Tonight I'll call my brother, Jeff, and we'll talk. I'll rent videos of funny movies and look forward to watching them. Maybe my "looking forward to" will be as simple as watching a Michigan State football game.

It came down to choice. Was I going to remain in a sea of hopelessness, or was I going to rebuild a positive anticipation of the future?

This matter of choice is paramount. After the loss of a loved one or a tragedy in life, we're thrown into a tailspin and a vortex of grief that seem irreversible. I thought a lot about my friend's challenge and realized I must believe that the best days of my life are still in front of me.

Viktor Frankl wrote:

No matter how difficult the path may be, the human spirit is only held back by choosing to give up, before it has had the chance to fly. Everyone has his own specific vocation or mission in life; everyone must carry out a concrete assignment that demands fulfillment. Therein he cannot be replaced, nor can his life be repeated, thus, everyone's task is unique as his specific opportunity to implement it. (*Man's Search for Meaning,* Beacon Press, 1959)

Frankl survived the terrors of the holocaust, when crusts of bread were a more precious commodity than any rare gem, and sunsets and starry skies were visions to be held close and cherished. In the midst of vile unjust torture, he learned the soul could yet be saturated with hope. Looking forward to the future for the best of one's life is the purest definition of hope I can imagine.

Wasn't that exactly what the Bible taught? I think of the number of saints who willingly gave up their lives through torture and imprisonment, looking forward to, as the Apostle Paul wrote, "the glory that lies ahead." Today countless men and women of faith are tortured for the sake of the gospel of Christ. I was able to witness the sacrifices of the Christian pastors in India. These brave, dedicated men and women lay their lives down every day willingly and gladly for the lives of others and for God.

I'm remembering a day near the end, when Patsy lay in bed, her life slowly ebbing away minute by minute, and she lifted her eyes to me and said in her frail voice, "Honey, when JonBenét died, she still had her baby teeth."

I lost my breath. Johnnie Bee had never lost a tooth. Patsy reached for my hand. "Read to me, John."

"Sure, sweetheart. What would you like me to read?"

"Psalms. Read the Psalms."

I read the Thirty-Fourth Psalm to her, and when I'd finished, I saw her lying there with tears swelling from her eyes.

"Oh, John, the Lord is near to those who have a broken heart..."

"Yes, and He promises to deliver them out of all their troubles."

"John?"

"Yes, darling."

"When is my next chemo treatment?"

I told her to rest, not to worry. "Soon," I lied. She sighed, smiled, and whispered, "Okay, good..." With the gentlest fluttering of her eyelids and a slight quiver of her lips, I think she understood. She wasn't afraid to die; she had already told me that. "You'll live, Patsy, you'll live and not die." She liked to make a joke of dying. "All the fun people are on the other side—my mom, Beth, JonBenét...no offense, John," and she would laugh.

At the end she didn't laugh. She didn't speak. She lay silent in her bed, absent from this world, her soul reaching for the arms of angels and far, far from me.

How was I going to find the best days before me?

CHAPTER 22

The Problem of Pride

*God can never trust His Kingdom
to anyone who has not been broken of pride,
for pride is the armor of darkness itself.*
—Francis Frangipane

On a Sunday noontime in Atlanta with a gentle Georgia breeze blowing through the tall pines, I sat on a bench by the church parking lot after the service before getting into my car. This was a new church Patsy and I had begun attending, and with her gone, I was getting used to going alone on Sunday mornings. Cars filed slowly out onto the street one after the other, and as I sat there, I watched a butterfly flutter around in front of me. A young man walked up to me, a bit nervous and anxious, and he stood by the bench, staring at me for an awkward moment.

"Mr. Ramsey...?"

I turned to face him. "Ah, hello," I said, recognizing him as one of the young men from the church.

"Excuse me, I wonder if I could talk to you?"

He was carrying a Bible. "Sure."

"You're not a reporter, are you?" I joked. "Sorry, just kidding! Sit down."

He sat next to me, fidgeting with his hands, mentioning the sermon, wasn't it good, yes, the pastor always preaches a good sermon, and wasn't this a nice day. I waited for him to get to the point.

"How do you do it?" he said at last.

"What do you mean?"

"Well, see, I got fired three months ago. I'm twenty-seven years old, and I've got a wife and a nine-month-old daughter." He stopped, scratched his head. "I don't know what I'm going to do."

"What's your line of work?"

"I'm a graphic designer. I worked at my company right out of art school and six years is a really long time to work in one place, but business fell off and I was a victim of downsizing. It was *unfair*."

Unfair.

"Where have you been looking for work?" I asked, watching the butterfly circle overhead.

"There's nothing out there in my field," he said with finality, "not that pays, anyhow."

I repeated, "But where have you been looking?"

He dropped his head. "That's just it. I stopped looking—I don't know what to do. My wife works a part-time job that barely pays minimum, and to pay for a sitter would take up her entire salary, so I'm home baby-sitting six hours a day for a nine-month-old."

"Have you thought of starting your own business? You could get a job just to pay bills doing anything at all, and in the meantime build up your own graphics design business."

His face fell. "Right. What kind of job should I get? Pumping gas? Waiting on tables?"

"Sure. Why not? Anything to bring some money in and pay the bills."

I thought of how I felt when General Electric took over my division at Lockheed Martin. The severance package, though I was grateful for it, didn't make up for the feeling of a lost identity.

"Sometimes I just want to run away," he said, his jaw tight.

I gave a sigh. "So what keeps you from doing it?"

He looked up, surprised. "Well, I love my wife! I love my baby! I can't just run away!"

"Ah. I see. I want to tell you something," I said. "I've made a lot of money in my life and I worked hard for it. I stumbled occasionally in business but always moved forward in the end. I was proud of my accomplishments, but never satisfied. Do you hear an operative word in what I just said?"

"Accomplishments?"

"No. The word is *proud.*"

His chin drew back into his neck. "Proud?"

"*Proud.* Pride can be a real roadblock to moving ahead. I didn't realize I was a proud man until I lost most everything. I had always thought of myself as humble, but I can see I was driven by pride. And here you are, a young, healthy guy, you've got a wife and child who love and need you, and you're just too proud to take menial work."

His face turned sullen. "You sound like my wife. That's what she tells me."

"Well?"

He took a deep breath, scratched his chin. "My wife's dad owns a produce company and he needs a guy right now to work on the loading dock stacking crates on trucks." He shot me a quick glance. "Would *you* take a job like that?"

I didn't hesitate to answer him. "If I had a family to feed? You bet I would. But first, the pride has to go. And to tell you the truth—"

An old station wagon with faded paint and a dented fender pulled out in front of us. A dad at the wheel laughing with his two boys in the back, and then a little girl with blond pigtails who looked like

JonBenét reached up to the front seat and gave her mother a hug.

"You were saying?" the young man said.

"To tell you the truth," I continued with a lump in my throat, "the Lord is still at work in me, helping me. I found out there are no shortcuts to getting back on your feet—and sanity."

Cars continued to slowly pull out of the church parking lot, families with children in the backseat, babies in car seats, families laughing and talking with one another.

"It takes time to rebuild a life, and even longer to reestablish hope for the future, my friend."

The parking lot was thinning out. "Look at that butterfly over there," I said. "Have you been watching it?"

He looked up, seeing the butterfly for the first time.

"Take a good look. That butterfly doesn't have a care in the world. It doesn't even realize how beautiful it is, it doesn't know how much pleasure it brings. We should be so carefree."

He laughed. "Wouldn't that be nice."

"I think we have to start meditating on the *goodness* of God," I said. "Life isn't always fair, but God is always good."

He smiled. "I have to get that into my head. My wife says I should stop feeling sorry for myself about losing my job. Maybe God has other plans for me."

"Of that I have no doubt."

He was quiet. Then holding his Bible, he said, "Will you pray for me?"

I reached over and clasped his shoulder. I prayed against a spirit of pride and asked the Lord to sovereignly reach down and give him the peace he craved. More than anything, I prayed he would learn to trust God, that he would place himself willingly into God's loving hands and trust Him completely for His sovereign goodness. I prayed for a deeper relationship with God, as I was discovering. I prayed for a new vision for him, new hope, work, and that he would see that his best days were ahead.

After a long silence, he said, "I actually feel better. I mean, why *not* take that job my father-in-law's got open? And why *not* start my own graphic design business? Maybe my wife and I could work together on it."

"Now you're talking. That's how I started out. My wife helped me run our business before we had enough money to hire other help."

He smiled, nodding his head. "It's worth thinking about."

By the time our conversation ended, the parking lot had emptied except for a few cars in the distance and the 911 Porsche parked at the end of the lot. I noticed it when I drove in, and now I knew without asking that the Porsche was his. He invited me to have dinner at his house; I told him thanks but I had other plans. Sometimes it's just too hard to look at yourself in someone else for too long.

CHAPTER 23

Getting Close to God

You are not truly free until you have lost everything.
—Aleksandr Solzhenitsyn

I was raised by a strong, determined dad who taught me, by example, to never give up, to find solutions to problems, to fix things that are broken, and to take responsibility. Engineering school taught me how to think logically and I learned in graduate business school to take time to get all the facts, to analyze a problem, and then to define a course of action. My philosophy in business was to never make a decision until I had to. I had believed that the words *I can't* were meant for other people, those people who didn't believe in themselves, the ones without self-esteem. After tragedy entered my life, self-doubt and defeating thoughts consumed me. I began thinking about all the things I had done wrong, all the wrong decisions I had made. My first marriage failed. I disrupted my family and moved to Boulder, Colorado, to pursue the almighty dollar. I made some incredibly bad business decisions after JonBenét was murdered. Decisions can fall into two categories, those that are permanent and those that can be reversed. Most decisions are *reversible*; a few are permanent and *irreversible*.

Sometimes making no decision is the best decision. Suffering can come from bad decisions we make, or can be caused by choices that others make. Suffering also results from the inherent risks of life. The insurance industry calls these "acts of God." That's really not fair to God.

I learned how suffering leads to depression, making each day a dread, as though life has stalled. For me, moving ahead meant focusing on creating new memories with my family and friends. My mind's RAM seems to have only a limited capacity for storing memories. When it's filled with old, sad memories, I become stalled, and I need to replace them with fresh, new, pleasant ones. I need to create new good memories to add to the good old ones.

I also know how much I need the Word of God in my life. I read the Psalms and the Proverbs. Many of the Psalms were written by King David, a great poet, who experienced enormous success, terrible suffering, and monumental failure and yet found joy, comfort, and relief in his relationship with God. The Book of Proverbs provides wisdom for everyday living and was written by King Solomon, son of David, whom God blessed with great wisdom. I try memorizing verses and reciting them over and over again. Spending time with God with regular prayer and Bible study became a lifesaver for me. If we don't work on getting our mind back, our prayers will remain desperate ones: "Help me, God!" "Why did You allow this, God?" "What am I supposed to do now, God?" will be our endless cries.

I didn't want my faith to remain a desperate kind of faith. I didn't want to stagnate in my woes, my communication with Heaven going up as pitiful pleas and sorrowful complaints. I wanted to know how Job did it; I wanted to be free to move ahead. I began to remind myself each morning that today is the first day of my new life and I will only focus on what is at hand for today.

The Bible tells us not to dwell on the past, as we cannot change it, and do not worry about the future and its potential problems because we have enough problems to deal with today. We're to focus on today. Future problems usually will not be as bad as we imagine them anyway.

Sorrow still sometimes yanks with its hooks in my chest and pulls. If you know what this is like, you know how you ache for relief, you want help, you want the hooks out of your chest. How I remember my girls' laughter, their radiant smiles, Beth, JonBenét, Patsy—lives cut short that could have given so much to this world, but God saw different.

I'm still here.

I've got to make my life count.

June 2009. I've traveled back to Michigan. I've just sold our home in Charlevoix, as the real estate market is in the midst of collapse. I have seller's remorse after the house sold. Selling that house is one of those irreversible decisions. I had intended to keep it until Burke graduated from college so he could have a house to come home to. Later when I had to sell it, I knew I had sold a source of memories and a refuge for Burke and me.

I still had my boat, though, a Matthews cabin cruiser, named *TenOClock*. It was built in 1962, of mahogany over oak, teak decks, and lots of varnished mahogany trim. *TenOClock* is small by today's boat standards, but it can sleep six if I open the sleeper sofa in the salon. With three hundred square feet of living space, it has a small compact galley, heads off each of the two sleeping quarters, and a salon area with a couch, an ottoman, and two upholstered chairs. When I bought the boat, I was convinced that Patsy, Burke, and I could live on the boat during the summer. It would be like a floating condo, I figured. That experiment lasted about three weeks. Patsy was a good sport through it all, but it was just too small. Now that I am alone, it has plenty of room.

I told a friend I had sold my house and was staying on my boat for the summer. He thought a minute and then laughed and said, "Hey, you're homeless!"

"No," I said, "just houseless."

It's summer, and the morning is clear and crisp above the cold waters of Lake Michigan. I rise early to watch the dawn erase the night over the lake when all is still except for the occasional fluttering gull squawking overhead and the gentle lap of the water against the wood hull. I sit on the aft deck now with my coffee, thinking about the day ahead and talking with God. The fresh smell of the summer air is filled with good memories. It reminds me of the days when my brother and

I scrambled to get our gear into the small cedar strip fishing boat to go fishing with Dad on Lake Mecosta. And I think of the mornings when John Andrew was young and beside me preparing for takeoff into the rising sun in our small airplane.

I stretch and rise to my feet to descend the five mahogany steps down to the sleeping quarters to get my Bible.

My home address now quietly sways with the waves beside the dock on Round Lake Harbor. Who would have thought twenty years ago—no, I can't go here. I shrug my shoulders and shake off the thought, pick up my Bible from the bedside table, and climb back up to the deck.

It will be here, living on my boat, where I'd learn what the ancient church fathers valued about solitude. Alone with God in stillness and simplicity. I don't have much to worry about these days. My goal is to move forward and hear from God. Now on the waters of Lake Michigan, with the summer days melting and silence surrounding me, I acknowledge it's time to enter this new phase of my life, the one where I learn the meaning of acceptance and surrender.

I discover what calms my soul, and how to turn off the churning of my mind. I discover how to rest in the peace of God. I continue to study the Bible, read Christian books, and learn more about prayer and intimacy with God. A friend gave me a copy of a little book on prayer by Martin Luther, penned in 1535, when his barber asked him for advice on how to pray. Luther wrote this small book to explain to his barber how he prayed each day. He explained in the book that he began by reading from the Psalms to quiet his mind. Then, he would recite the Lord's Prayer; "Our Father, who art in Heaven..." Then he would recite the Ten Commandments: "I shall have one God, I shall have no false idols..." Then he would recite the Apostles' Creed: "I believe in one God, maker of all things seen and unseen..." Then and only then would Luther begin his personal conversation with God.

Luther spent hours each morning with this prayer ritual. It's a good spiritual discipline and gets my day started off better. I don't spend hours in prayer like Luther, often just a half hour. I'm finding thoughts in the Bible I never knew were there. Thoughts from the Book of Job: "For there is hope for a tree, If it is cut down, that it will sprout again, And that its tender shoots will not cease" (Job 14:7), which speaks to me of rebirth and rebuilding the future.

I wish I could adequately explain what happens inside me when I spend time with God. The Word of God lifts me up and gives me a sense of tranquillity. It's like drinking cool, fresh water when you're parched. I'm much more at peace. My bruised and battered spirit is being healed.

I pray a lot these days. Not long prayers. I pray while replacing the air horn on the boat, I pray while walking to the bookstore. I pray while boiling water for coffee. Short prayers, but prayers nevertheless. I read about a man who tried to talk to God once every minute of every waking hour, even if it was just to say "Hi, God, I know you're there." I tried it for a while, too.

A friend of mine told a story about himself. He decided he would pray for thirty minutes each day, so the first day he set a timer, and began praying. He prayed for everyone he could think of—our leaders, our country, his family, neighbors; he prayed for all the things he needed. When he totally exhausted everything he could pray about, he looked at the timer, and only three-and-one-half minutes had elapsed.

I don't think God cares about the length of our prayers but I do think He cares that we come to Him often each day.

Night on the boat in the harbor brings a different kind of peace than the morning. Occasionally before crawling into my small bunk, I walk to the end of the dock and watch the calm water and distant lights across the harbor. I can see the twinkling lights from the windows of houses in my old neighborhood. The photographers and tabloid reporters are gone now. Yes, life does get better and problems do fade into the past. I breathe in the cool summer night air and look up in amazement at the nearness of the stars against the indigo Michigan sky. I shrug off a mosquito, and I thank God. I can thank God for life. I can smile. Life can be good again.

CHAPTER 24

Learning Discipleship

There are many plans in a man's heart, Nevertheless the LORD's counsel—that will stand.
—Proverbs 19:21

Taking five months out of my life to spend time getting to know God was not a decision I made casually. My good friends, Dr. Jim and Jan Conway and other friends, had been encouraging me for months to take the five months necessary to go to the WYAM Discipleship Training School, and then on a mission trip to India. They promised it would be life changing, but I just couldn't see myself as a missionary.

I couldn't imagine taking five months out of my

life, away from family and friends, the Internet, Starbucks, and hot showers. But there I was, three months later, in a dusty TATA SUV, on a potholed highway outside the city of Chitradurga, India, cutting through mountainous rock formations, rice paddies, and sugarcane fields. Chitradurga lies at the base of a chain of high peaks where massive gray granite boulders are strewn randomly about the landscape. Hundreds of crude, brightly painted trucks clog the road carrying iron ore to the coast to be shipped to China. Intermixed with the speeding trucks are shepherds herding their goats and cows while ox-pulled carts loaded with sugarcane cuttings disrupt the flow of traffic. Accidents are frequent, usually a head-on collision involving two iron ore–laden trucks.

We're a group of fifteen Americans, South Koreans, Australians, and South Africans, and we've been together for four months now, having spent the first three at the Youth With A Mission Discipleship Training School in Kona, Hawaii. We're now here in India to support local Indian pastors and help them with their work in the small villages populated primarily by poor, untouchable caste people, most of whom are Hindu.

We're headed to our next base of operations in the city of Belgaum, India, nestled in the foothills of the Western Ghats. Belgaum is a small city by

India standards: five million people, plus or minus. We will be staying at a former orphanage built by the British in the late 1880s. Local Indian pastors have been working for years to restore the stone and tile-roofed buildings to serve as a Christian retreat center. They welcome us gladly and are proud to show us that we will have cots to sleep on, a luxury not afforded to guests previously. There is cold running water, which is fed by a cistern on top of the building. Hot water will come from the cooking fire in one-gallon buckets.

Upon our arrival, we are treated to a meal of curry and rice and *nam,* Indian flat bread, and after dinner, we sit around the coals of the cooking fire and discuss what lies ahead. Each day we will visit three to four villages, some as many as four hours apart.

In the morning I fill a one-gallon plastic bucket from a fifty-gallon pot of hot water sitting on the cooking fire. Alternating between soap, cold water, and scoops from the hot water bucket, my shower is as good as any in a five-star hotel. We eventually get our two SUVs loaded. To sit in the front with the Indian driver is the prime seat but also puts you closest to the scene of an accident, which seems imminent at all times. I preferred to sit in the back and not see the hazards ahead. Sometimes denial is great protection from danger.

After several hours on the rutted roads, we arrive at the first village of the day. The eager faces of women and children greet us. The children are the most excited. They reach out their hands to shake ours. The women and children assemble in a clearing in the center of the village on straw mats, and the men of the village, who look at us with skepticism, stand at the rear of the gathering. The host pastor explains who we are and that we're there to show them God's love. Our team has developed little skits and games for the children, and the children laugh and clap along as the games progress. It is remarkable to me that these kids relate to what is going on, even though they don't understand our language.

The village, like all the others we visit, is populated by Dalits, the lowest Hindu caste, commonly called Untouchables. It is estimated that there are two hundred and fifty million "untouchable" men, women, and children in India. These people are doomed to generations of poverty by a Hindu system of social discrimination. Hindus believe that they are born into the untouchable caste because they have sinned in a previous life and therefore must serve a penance for their sins in this lifetime. If they live life well as a Dalit, they will be born into a higher caste level in the next life. Each lifetime without sin, you move to a higher caste. The highest caste is a Brahmin. A devout Hindu, at the Brahmin level, lives a privileged life, and prays to come back in the next life as a cow, the highest God in the Hindu religion. Some Dalits have realized they can break out of the caste system by converting to Christianity or Islam, but evangelism in India is against the law.

A little girl about eight or nine years old sits on a makeshift board with homemade wheels. She appears to have cerebral palsy, unable to walk, her arms flailing about. She's dressed in a clean cotton dress with a purple ribbon holding her hair from her forehead. I can see she's loved and cared for just like the other children of the village whose proud mothers are always nearby. This child's mother gets the attention of our interpreter. The interpreter leans over to me. "She's asking you to pray for her child."

As a father of three daughters, I have a special place in my heart for girls. This child tugs at my heart because despite her severe handicaps, a certain innocence shines through her face.

But it's customary in India that only women should pray for females.

Did she really mean she wanted me to pray?

The interpreter nods. "Yes, please."

I kneel on the straw mat before the girl. I'm not sure what to say as I take her hand, which is callused from propelling her makeshift wheelchair, and I look into her large, imploring, brown eyes. The women of our group gather around us, scarves draped over their heads, and they pray. Their voices rise and fall in prayer over this child on a skateboard with her twisted little body in the cotton dress. Her head turns, her body contorts, but the look on her face is one of delight.

"Lord, touch this child..." I pray.

The palsied girl becomes calmed and quiet. I want her to speak, to get to her feet, but I don't know what God will do. She didn't change before our eyes but I know God heard our prayers.

A man pushes his way through the crowd and brings his ten-year-old son forward for prayer and places him in front of me. Our interpreter tells me he has stomach cancer and will be going back to the doctor next week. This young boy's stomach is fully distended and rock hard. I kneel down and place my hand on his warm stomach. I start to pray.

A flurry of movement around us. Voices crying out. Others drawing together around the boy and praying.

"Lord," I begin, "You say You've given each of us the authority to pray in Your name, and that we will be able to do what You have done plus more. I therefore declare that this child of Yours is healed by the power You have given me!" (I'm not sure if I'm saying the right words but I try my best.) The father thanks us and steps back into the crowd with the boy, who seems to have a hopeful smile.

Things get hectic. A woman comes forward and hands me a plastic water bottle. I think she's giving me water to drink, but she explains to our interpreter she wants me to bless the water. I'm confused. Bless the water? But I pray a blessing over the bottle of water, not wanting to offend her. More hurting men and women ask for prayer. A lady bends down in the dirt and tries to kiss my foot. I'm shocked and quickly raise her up telling her, "No no. I'm only a fellow follower of Jesus. Please, no!" Another woman presses a 100-rupee bill into my hand. My interpreter quickly explains to her that we don't want to take money. Apparently the Hindu priests expect to be paid when they pray for someone.

The needs of the people are beyond my comprehension. I'm overcome with their pleas for prayers, their desperate faces. When we leave, the children surround our vehicles, pressing against the windows, reaching for our hands. They run alongside the truck calling our names; some follow us on bicycles. I've had so much all my life and was ignorant of the rest of the world. This is truly an awakening. How is it I've been so blind? Each day we return exhausted from our travels to these villages and don't know if our prayers for these poor villagers will be answered, but we do take comfort knowing that God has heard them.

Two weeks later we received word that the boy with stomach cancer went to the doctor, and no cancer was found in his body.

My friends were right. My life will never be the same.

CHAPTER 25

Dream of Flying

*Adversities do not make a man fail,
they show what kind of man he is.*
—Thomas à Kempis

I've always liked airplanes and flying ever since I was six years old when my dad started teaching me to be his copilot. Ask any pilot, and when pressed, they will admit that flying is an addiction. Once flying gets in your blood, you always want it. It may be the freedom of three-dimensional movement, it may be the speed, it may be the exhilaration of winding through clouds and seeing things that the earthbound cannot see.

For a long time, the only way I could afford to

fly was to belong to a flying club, where many people shared a few airplanes and paid dues and an hourly fee to use the club plane. The planes weren't always the best equipped and were usually worn around the edges but mechanically were in good shape. My dad had taught me how to fly and helped me get my private pilot license. After I went through a fair amount of additional flight training and passed the exam for my commercial multiengine and instrument flight instructor licenses, I felt pretty confident—maybe even a bit cocky.

Our club had an old single-engine Cessna 182 and I flew it all over the country, sometimes for family trips and occasionally for business.

One day in June, I had decided to fly down to Cocoa Beach, Florida, for a dinner meeting. Two hours after takeoff, I landed at the Cocoa Beach airport and taxied up to the fuel service, but it was closed, so I tied the airplane down, thinking I'd refuel the next morning.

The next morning was a typical humid summer morning in Florida. Not much weather to worry about, other than the pop-up thunderstorms forecasted for later in the day, routine occurrences that time of year. I banged on the door of the fuel service office but it was still closed. I calculated that I had enough fuel in the plane's tanks to make it back to Atlanta. I wasn't thinking of the old axiom in flying that goes, "The only time you have too much fuel is when the plane is on fire."

I took off with half-empty fuel tanks, but the weather seemed fair enough and I figured the straight shot up to Atlanta should be a piece of cake. However, the pop-up thunderstorms began forming earlier than I had expected, and my planned direct route to Atlanta became a twisted path. I was forced to wander all over southern Georgia to avoid the storms, and now my fuel supply was barely adequate.

About forty miles from my Atlanta destination, I realized I wasn't going to make it. I had to land somewhere, and I had to do it pretty quickly or I would run out of fuel.

The navigation equipment in the old airplane was marginal at best. I contacted Atlanta Approach Control on the radio and asked for a radar vector to the Carrollton airport, which was the nearest landing field. They told me they were too busy, so I was on my own. As I headed toward where I thought the Carrollton airport should be, I tried to find a suitable open landing field within gliding distance, because I knew the engine could quit at any moment. Suddenly, Georgia seemed to have much more forested land than open fields.

The engine quit, and now landing was a requirement, not an option. I approached a plowed field below, careful to stay in close and preserve precious altitude. On final approach to the field, I turned the control wheel hard to the left and depressed the right rudder nearly to the floor, causing the airplane to slip sideways and lose altitude rapidly. Just before touching down, I straightened out the controls and I touched down on the plowed field. The airplane shook as the small wheels passed over the freshly plowed furrows. The plane came to a quick stop.

It was very quiet. (No need to shut the engine off. It had shut itself off minutes earlier.) The landing was one I could have bragged about to my pilot friends, except for the fact that I had run out of fuel. If the engine had failed owing to a cracked cylinder or a broken rod, I could have boasted for years how I'd expertly landed in a farmer's field with no harm done to the airplane. But this! I couldn't tell anyone about it because any pilot who runs out of fuel is considered to be a fool, or worse.

I climbed out of the cockpit to meet a wide-eyed farmer in overalls, high boots, and straw hat standing on the baseboard of his truck. He may have asked if I was hurt. He may have asked if I was from Mars. He may have offered me a chaw of tobacco and a swig of something from an unlabeled jug, I don't know. I was shaken and disgusted with myself. I wanted to back up my day a few hours and wait for the fuel service in Cocoa Beach to open, refuel, and start the trip over again. I had made one of those *irreversible* decisions and it bit me hard.

"Any chance I could get a ride to the nearest airport to get some fuel?" I asked, my voice sounding coarse with the adrenaline rush parching my throat.

"Well, I reckon, son. You hurt?"

"No sir. Just out of fuel."

"Well, that was some landing you made there. Why didn't you land at the Carrollton airport? It's only about three miles away."

Three miles.

I offered to pay him for any damage I'd done to his new crops, and he nodded his approval, becoming a bit friendlier. I could never tell my dad about this.

I was hoping it wouldn't become a big deal in that little town in Georgia where I guess not much exciting happened, at least nothing like a small aircraft dropping out of the sky onto an alfalfa field. I felt like the pilot Saint-Exupéry, in one of John Andrew's books, *The Little Prince*. Any minute one of the kids was bound to ask me "If you please, draw me a sheep?" I should have been wearing a leather cap with earflaps, hip boots, and a leather flight jacket, not my business suit with a briefcase in the backseat. A few neighbors joined the party and the farmer loaded me in his truck and I left for the Carrolton airport for fuel.

I poured the 15 gallons of fuel in the wing tanks using a borrowed ladder and, with the help of the farmer and his neighbors, pushed the airplane into position for takeoff. I bade the farmer and the bevy of his friends and neighbors farewell, thanked them for their hospitality, and I was on my way.

I landed at DeKalb-Peachtree Airport later that evening, tied the airplane down, cleaned the grass stains off the prop tips, got in my car, and decided to quit flying forever.

I hadn't flown an airplane for two years when in 1986 the movie *Top Gun* came out. I decided to go see it because it was about flying, but I didn't expect it to inspire me to fly again. I sat absorbed in the aerial action in this film about a naval aviator aboard the aircraft carrier USS *Enterprise*, played by Tom Cruise. He has to regain his confidence after a fatal training accident, and the main thing I loved were the flight scenes. I was a pilot, too, wasn't I? Maybe I could trust myself to fly again.

I came home from the movie inspired and, with Patsy's consent, did something radical: I bought my first airplane, a 1966 twin-engine Beechcraft Baron. I decided that I would fly again only if

I could maintain the airplane and the navigation equipment at high standards. No more flying club rentals with nonoperating navigation equipment.

Throughout the years I've bought and sold several planes, including my last plane, a Beechcraft V35 Bonanza, which I co-owned with a partner. I sold my share of the Bonanza to my partner in 2010 and left the flying life. I felt as if I had lost an old friend who had taken me through countless storms and delivered me safely home each time. Flying doesn't leave the blood. I remember when my dad gave up flying one day, and I always wondered if he missed it. I wish I had asked him because I still have a dream to one day own another airplane. That thought is part of my enthusiasm for the future.

I can still dream.

CHAPTER 26

Changing Perspectives

Do not fear death so much, but rather the inadequate life.
—Bertolt Brecht

On a commercial flight from Atlanta to New York, the Christmas season was in full swing. I was seated next to a man who introduced himself as a retired radio personality. I apologized for not recognizing his name. "I don't pay attention to the media much anymore," I explained.

The flight attendant had just served me some coffee and I was putting on my headset. "What are you listening to?" my seatmate asked.

"Oldies but goodies if I can find them. I'm a product of the sixties," I said.

"I don't listen to music much anymore. It used to be my business but now it gets me down."

Was he talking about all music or just certain kinds of music?

"I hate Christmas music, but the real truth is, I don't like any music," he grumbled.

I looked at his face to see if he was serious. I had never met anyone who didn't like music of any kind. I find music to be soothing and healing. It helps me focus my thoughts on good things.

"Wait a minute," he said with sudden recognition. "You said your name is—well! Are you *the* John Ramsey?"

"Afraid so."

"Well, then you know a little something about better times, eh?" He sighed, shook his head. "For me, and I'm sure for you, Christmas is the worst. Reminds me of when my wife was alive..." He paused, opened the little bottle of bourbon on his tray. "You probably think I sound like a bitter old man."

I removed the headset. "Christmas used to be very difficult for me," I said, "particularly Christmas music."

"So you know how I feel."

I stirred the small plastic cup of creamer into my coffee and said, "I guess I've just always taken music for granted."

"Ha! Taken music for granted. So much we take for granted, and then one day it's too late. It's gone before we know it." He poured the liquor into the small plastic cup filled with ice.

I took a sip of my coffee and the thought came to me that this flight might just turn out to be a very long one. I usually like to sleep on flights and rarely talk much to those around me. On and on the man went, lamenting about the past and happier times. He seemed to feel life was pretty much finished because the good old days were over. I guess he was accustomed to talking a lot since he was a radio commentator and I was his captive audience.

Finally, I spoke up. "I can understand your missing your life when it was better. I've learned that missing the past so much can prevent us from finding contentment in the present, and hope for the future.

"Something had to change," I said, taking the last swallow of coffee, "or I was going to become one of those mean-spirited old guys in the back pew of the church growling about what's wrong with the world. I didn't want to live my life in the past, wounded and bitter."

We talked about men our age who have known a level of fame or success based on worldly measurements, and after we pass the peak of what we have been striving for, it becomes important to redefine success. It's more difficult to define because it's not based on accumulation of assets or increasingly better job titles. We must turn our attention inward and focus on what difference we really have made in the world. I explained that faith played a big part in my view of the future. I told him that I believe God has a purpose for each of us as long as we are alive.

I mentioned my trip to India, and how it had changed my perspective on life.

"I've been there. Changed your perspective on life? How so?"

I told him about the old man outside the Delhi Airport, and about the little girl with cerebral palsy. I mentioned the demonic atmosphere I had felt at the Yellamma Temple.

"The Yellamma Temple? Never heard of it. Tell me about it."

I took a breath and began. "Yellamma is the name of a female goddess worshipped by millions of poor Hindu Indians. Her followers take a vow to dedicate themselves, their wives, and often their female children to serve the Goddess Yellamma in hopes that they will be blessed in return.

"Young girls dedicated to Yellamma live a life of servitude for their whole lives, and often as prostitutes, as their act of service to the goddess. I was told there are over two hundred thousand of these temple women in India."

"Two hundred thousand, good grief!"

"And they have no hope whatsoever of a normal life. I wouldn't believe it if I hadn't seen it."

Now I was the one with the captive audience.

I told him how our group visited the temple the day before worshippers were to gather. "The temple is located at Soudathi, only a few hours from the city of Belgaum. We drove the rough roads until we saw a single mountain rise up on the horizon above the surrounding flat land with the temple at the very top. It was a strange sight.

"On the mountainside road our SUV passed caravans of hundreds of painted carts, each drawn by single oxen, heading to the mountaintop."

"Hundreds."

"Oh, thousands were on their way. Their oxen were adorned with red, yellow, orange, and blue ribbons, and clanking bells; their horns were painted with blue and yellow paint, quite colorful, yet sad."

"I can picture it."

I went on. "In twenty-four hours, three hundred thousand people would gather at this mountain temple site for the semiannual dedication of two thousand new temple servants, mostly young women."

"My God!"

"Exactly. That's what I pray, my God! These dedications occur in India only on the day of a full moon, which, for me, added to the feeling of evil."

I became more animated as I spoke. "I tell you, I felt my stomach turn as we witnessed this awful thing. Later we had the opportunity to minister to twenty or so of the older women who've served Yellamma their whole lives. We served them a good, healthy meal, and had the opportunity to share how God loved them. These women can never marry, most have AIDS, and they are not fed or clothed by the temple. After they're dedicated, they return to their villages to a life of begging and servitude. They told us, their only hope is a hope to die."

"Dreadful," said the man beside me.

"We arrived at Yellamma and parked near one of three large bathing pools at the entrance to the temple. Thousands of people were already gathered around the pool, immersing themselves in preparation for their visit up to the holy site. They had either red or yellow paint on their foreheads, the color signifying whether they are male or female devotees. Men and women both were dressed in colorful silk saris, turbans, veils, and abundant jewelry. You'd think they were celebrating something happy, something wonderful, a wedding maybe."

"Just dreadful," said the man.

"And there were men devotees who were dressed as women, and paid to bless cars as they pass because those blessings are considered to be meaningful by the worshippers. He didn't bless ours. We must have looked very out of place in our sunglasses, western clothes, and tennis shoes, but the worshippers paid no attention to us. Sitting there I really had the feeling that evil was very near in this bizarre place."

"I saw poverty, but nothing like this..." said the man, rubbing his eye.

"But the temple itself!" I said, continuing my story. "The temple itself was a single-story concrete block building. Fairly indistinguishable outside. It looked more like a large, run-down high school football stadium locker room, not what you'd think of as a religious temple. Yellow and red powder thrown by devotees was splashed against every square inch of the building walls. It looked like children had made a terrible mess with house paint. But then! Oh, then!"

"What? What then?"

"I saw a young girl who probably was in her early twenties crawling on her stomach up the hill to the entrance of the temple. Several old ladies sprinkled water before her as she slithered along, her body never more than a few inches from the ground. She had a look of sadness and despair. She was to be dedicated, forced into servitude for the rest of her life."

"I have a daughter. That's awful—"

"I had heard of demonic oppression but didn't give much credence to it. Now I sensed it strongly, and let me tell you, it was overwhelming. It was hell itself."

"I thought that type of thing was outlawed in India," said the man, and swallowed the last of his bourbon.

"It is, but it still goes on," I told him.

"Right. Like child trafficking. Makes you sick," he said with a mumble.

We were quiet, listening to the hum of the airplane, and then he said, "Did your experience help you recognize the good things in your life?"

"Yes," I said, "it certainly did."

Memories of India will forever burn in my head. The Indian people I met were kind, industrious, intelligent, and gentle, but as a Westerner, I had a hard time understanding the spiritual practices. Twenty percent of the world's poor live in India, a country of more than a billion people. It's a culture that has been alive for more than a thousand years, and religious practices have been ingrained in the population.

I wasn't aware how long I talked. The man beside me had watched my face and listened intently as I spoke. He said nothing more, just sat, staring out the window.

We landed at LaGuardia and he gave me a warm handshake. "Merry Christmas, John. I hope you have a merry Christmas—and thanks. You've made me think." He shook my hand again, gave a smile and a nod, and disappeared into the crowd. I walked along the walkway of one of the world's most congested airports, remembering the chaos and pungent smells of the Delhi airport. But here there was no crippled, old Indian man coiled on a rug grinning up at me, as though he had been waiting all his life to be noticed.

CHAPTER 27

Are Demons Real?

*Be strong in the Lord and in the power of His might.
Put on the whole armor of God, that you may be able to stand against the wiles of the devil.*
—Ephesians 6:10–11

My mission trip to India was an eye-opener for me in terms of experiencing a more spiritual world. I never gave much credence to the possibility that people could be demon possessed. In our increasingly secular surroundings, we focus on what is seen and not what is unseen, as the Bible warns us not to do.

While we do not look at the things which are seen, but at the things which are not seen. For the

things which are seen are *temporary, but the things which are not seen* are *eternal.*
—2 Corinthians 4:18

I saw the tremendous demonic influence in human lives at the Yellamma Temple, on the streets of Belgaum, in some of the remote villages we visited. I witnessed prayers of Christian believers exorcise evil from tormented people. I have to admit, I wouldn't have believed it if I hadn't seen it with my own eyes.

Here's what the Bible says about the origin of Satan, or evil:

How you are fallen from heaven,
  O Lucifer, son of the morning!
  How you are cut down to the ground,
  You who weakened the nations!
  For you have said in your heart:
  'I will ascend into heaven,
  I will exalt my throne above the
  stars of God;
  I will also sit on the mount of the
  congregation
  On the farthest sides of the north;
  I will ascend above the heights of
  the clouds,

I will be like the Most High.'
—Isaiah 14:12–14

The Bible is full of warnings about demonic activity in the spiritual world. I believe these warnings are just as applicable today as they were in biblical times. My experience in India opened my eyes to a culture which is very spiritually aware and where the spirit world is much more accepted and commonplace than in the Western world. I realized it was naïve and ill-informed to ignore the reality of the demonic realm as we go about our lives.

The above verses explain how the devil fell from God's presence in Heaven. He wanted to be like God! And God said:

Yet you shall be brought down to Sheol,
  To the lowest depths of the Pit.
—Isaiah 14:15

The Book of Ezekiel records that Satan was once a beautiful angel, but he fell from grace because of his pride. He had it all and he blew it, which is what he wants us to do. Blow it. His goal is to get humans to join him in defeat.

Suffering comes at us when we least expect it. Suddenly it's here upon us, and we simply must reach out to God for His light. He has given us His authority to dispel the black cloud that so easily traps us. Because of His authority, we can begin to contend for our lives.

And Jesus came and spoke to them, saying, "All authority has
   been given to Me in heaven and on earth."
—Matthew 28:18
Behold, I give you the authority to trample on serpents and scorpions, and over all the power of the enemy.
—Luke 10:19

I'm fully aware that God does allow us to go through trials, persecution, and suffering for a divine purpose. I see now how suffering humbles us. Suffering makes us open to the pain of others, and I'm beginning to see that what I've been through gives me a unique empathy to help others through the same pain. I'm speaking from the other side of suffering now. When I comprehend what He's done for me, I can say, "Okay, Lord, it is well with my soul."

For most of my life I wondered if the account of Adam and Eve in Genesis was a myth, or possibly a metaphor for something else, but I now believe its true and potent message. Satan's deceitful influence convinced Adam and Eve that they could be like God—all-knowing—and sinful human pride entered the world. I now believe demonic activity is very real.

God is far more powerful than evil powers, and we are promised in Psalms 91 that He sends His angels to watch over us, protect us, help us. Even as I write these words, I can't help getting a tight feeling in my stomach as I think of my JonBenét and the times I asked the Lord after her death, were her guardian angels surrounding her?

God answered me.

John, I was there, and her angels were there, just as when My Son was nailed on the cross—legions of angels surrounded Him. No child of Mine is ever alone at the hour of death.

I heard His words in my heart and I embraced them.

> Dear Lord, I lay down my life before You.
> If the way ahead is difficult, I thank You
> that we'll go through it together.
> I take a stand now against all demonic
> influences and curses against my life in
> the name of Jesus. I thank you for
> opening my eyes, for giving me eyes

to see and ears to hear You. I was so
blind. I thought living a decent life was
enough for You. Forgive me for taking
so long to come Home. I no longer place
my life in the fickle hands
of human approval...
I'm trusting you to guide me and
use me for Your purposes for
the remainder of my life. Amen.

CHAPTER 28

A Man's Legacy

*Strive not to be a success,
But rather be of value.*
—Albert Einstein

In the summer of 2010, I received a searing jolt. Lou Smit, my friend, and one of the keys for finding JonBenét's killer, died. I admired Lou because he did what he believed was right regardless of popular opinion or peer pressure. He believed in our innocence and refused to let the case go cold. "I will get this guy! I'll get him, John. I'm sure of it," and I was confident he would do just that. We liked Lou Smit from the moment we first met. He told us, "I've been criticized for believing in your innocence because you're Christians, but I've put lots of Christians behind bars."

Based on his scrutiny of the case and his seasoned detective's eye, he believed, as we knew, that an intruder had killed our daughter. Lou fought for what was right and would not let the system trample us, even though he was going against a tide of popular opinion. He worked selflessly on the case for more than fourteen years. During that time we got to know each other well, and my appreciation and admiration for him grew exponentially. He was a real detective and a real man.

In May 2010, he called and invited me to meet him in Colorado for a couple of days of golf, but unfortunately, I was unable to go. "I'll make it next time, Lou."

But there would be no next time. The last e-mail I received from Lou explained he had some serious surgery coming up, but he didn't elaborate. I didn't want to pry, and I knew Lou did not exaggerate. He seemed fit as a racehorse, though he had dealt with prostate cancer a few years before. He treated it like most people treated a common cold. No big deal.

When I finally was able to get in touch with Lou, he explained, "Cancer is back, but it's just a bump in the road. That's how it goes, my friend."

The next thing I knew, he was in hospice.

I flew to Colorado immediately to sit by his side. This man who had stood up for us and in many respects saved our lives lay prostrate in bed with tubes and wires connected to his body. He still talked in his strong resonant voice. "John, I'm afraid as long as the case remains in the hands of the Boulder police, it may never be solved." It was the first time I ever heard him doubt that the case would be solved. He went on to tell me about leads, what needed to be done, who should be looked at in depth. He said, "I guess I won't find out who the murderer is until I see JonBenét in Heaven." His strength was waning but his humor and positive outlook were not. "I'm not afraid to go, John, but I just wish I could have caught this guy first."

Lou had lost his wife two years before Patsy died, and we occasionally compared notes on being widowers. Lou joked from his hospice bed that dating was a lot of work and maybe he would just give it up for a while. His last words to me as I left his room were, "John, I'll see you later." I knew what he meant.

Yes, Lou. I will see you later.

Lou's family asked me to speak at his funeral on behalf of all the crime victims he'd helped. Lou had solved two hundred murders in his career and by doing so helped families bring closure to a tragic event in their lives. I was honored beyond words. What do you say about someone who accomplished so much and stood for what was right, despite the odds and criticism?

I drove into the church parking lot that sad morning and was impressed by the spotless white police motorcycles lined up with precision, ready for the police honor guard in their crisp dress uniforms to lead the procession to the gravesite. The church was filled with people who knew and respected Lou.

At the back of the church were two hundred pairs of shoes, one pair on each seat, symbolizing the two hundred victims for whom Lou had found justice. I approached the open casket, and at the sight of him lying there, this dear, great man, I burst into tears. I didn't expect to cry because I'd been exposed to so much loss, but there I was, sobbing uncontrollably. I couldn't stop until I moved away from the casket.

My son John Andrew stood next to me, which helped. Having him there with me, my son who was no longer a boy, but a man, wanting to show his respect for Lou as much as I did.

Then came time for me to speak. I stood at the podium and catching my breath, I spoke from my heart.

Here's my message in part:

It is very much an honor to share in the celebration of Lou Smit's life and to share my thoughts about Lou...

Lou was to take a fair amount of heat in the media for praying with us, but I was to learn that Lou was very capable of withstanding any amount of heat aimed his way.

When I think of Lou and what he did, I'm reminded of that well-known quote of Irish philosopher Edmund Burke: "All that is necessary for evil to triumph is for good men to do nothing." Lou was a good man who courageously stepped forward in front of a tidal wave of opinion in our case...

As time progressed, Lou showed me by example what a real detective was. I would often tell people that Lou was a real-life Colombo and Dirk Pitt all rolled into one...

Lou's end objective was the absolute pursuit of truth so that justice in its finest sense would prevail...Dr. John Douglas, the person who established the FBI profiling program a number of years ago...said to me, "If I had done something wrong, I certainly wouldn't want that guy on my tail."

I had the opportunity to visit Lou for a few hours shortly after he went into hospice and a week before he died...Lou believed that as one charged with bringing justice for the victim of a crime, he must stand in their shoes and fight for them, because they cannot... We talked as if it was any other day in Lou's life...

Remarkably during that time together Lou talked a lot about the case, what needed to be done next. He wasn't about to quit and give up... and he talked about the exciting journey that lay before him.

Many men strive for the legacy Lou left; few succeed. I'm sure that when Lou arrived in Heaven, God welcomed him and said, "Well done, good and faithful servant. You have accomplished all that I lay before you. Welcome home."

I walked out of the church that day knowing I had lost a real friend. But even without Lou, we have not reached the end of the road in the search for my daughter's killer. Thank God there are other dedicated men and women who volunteered their time alongside Lou on the case, and I know they won't quit the search. Now Lou has solved his last case; I just wish he could share the answer from Heaven.

CHAPTER 29

Stopping the Fall

Now faith is the substance of things hoped for, the evidence of things not seen.
—Hebrews 11:1

Reentering life after tragedy or loss can be extremely difficult. Years of investment in building a business, home, career, or marriage that is suddenly lost can make the thought of rebuilding overwhelming. Before beginning to rebuild, it is necessary to first *stop the fall*. Like an airplane descending powerlessly to the ground, the first step is to get the plane leveled off and get the airspeed stabilized. Only then is the objective to start climbing again.

After JonBenét was murdered, a good friend cautioned me, "John, be careful, your sword is now dull." What he was saying was that my normally clear mind and good decision-making capabilities were impaired. The problem was, I didn't know it, and despite my friend's wise advice, I went on to make many poor decisions. Our ability to make good decisions is damaged after tragedy, because we are not thinking clearly. The best thing I could have done was to put my life in park for a while. I was eager to start climbing again and didn't realize I hadn't stopped the fall yet.

Here are some suggestions for stopping the fall, the first being, and if you get no other point of advice from this book, please hear this one: After you have suffered a tragic circumstance in your life, press the pause button *and put your life on hold*. Do not make any big decisions or moves. Focus on stopping the fall first. Realize also that this "life hold" will be necessary for longer than you think.

One way I needed to stop the fall was in the area of finances. Unfortunately, many victims of violent crime end up financially devastated because of legal expenses, poor business decisions, disrupted careers, carelessness with money, and divorce. I should have begun downsizing and protecting my savings at a much more aggressive rate than I did. I just assumed things would get back to normal quickly. Money for legal expenses was going out like water through a fire hose. On and on and on the expenses mounted at a time when I should have been preserving every penny. My expenses were simply out of control.

At a minimum, accept that your decision-making ability is damaged and try to avoid making any big decisions, particularly financial ones. Always seek the counsel of a friend or relative. Most important, listen to them. I had good advice that I chose not to listen to because I thought I was perfectly capable of making good decisions, just like always. The best thing I could have done was swallow my pride and reach out to a trusted friend and say "I need your help. I'm afraid I'm not making good decisions. Here is my checkbook. I will not make any decisions without consulting you, and I need you to be forceful with me. Help take control of my life for a while, please." It's a lot to ask of a friend, but that's what is needed.

If your tragedy involves the legal system, act quickly to seek good legal counsel. Don't hire a real estate attorney if it's a criminal matter. If you are guilty of a crime, you must have a lawyer to make sure you are treated fairly. If you are innocent, you must have a great lawyer to make sure you are not wrongly convicted. To ensure that the system is just, you must be able to afford to defend yourself, if necessary. You can be sure you are treated justly, but it is very expensive. Those who can't afford to defend themselves properly are in much more danger of being wrongly convicted if the system is in the hands of biased individuals.

There are eighteen thousand police jurisdictions in the United States—most are competent, but some are not. Small police departments cannot possibly have experience to deal with every circumstance, yet in most cases, they have total authority over investigating crimes committed in their jurisdiction. Qualified help is available to them, but only if they ask for it.

England has eight jurisdictions and is considering reducing them to six to ensure that every jurisdiction has competency and experience in all matters.

Police will often say, "Innocent people don't need attorneys, and if you hire an attorney, you must be guilty." That has been proven wrong countless times. A mistake I made in those early hours after finding JonBenét missing was to assume the police knew what they were doing. I should have escalated things on my own initiative. I should have called anyone and everyone I knew who could possibly bring resources and attention to bear on finding JonBenét. I learned early in my business career with AT&T that if you have a problem and it's not getting resolved, escalate it to the next higher level, and then the next, and the next until all resources are focused on getting your problem fixed.

I suggest using this turning point in your life to simplify and downsize. It's human nature to accumulate things, to want comfort. So what do we do? We buy things, even things we don't need. These things can be huge burdens, and after tragedy, the burden of too much stuff can sink you emotionally, if not financially. It's not easy to do. Sell what you can, give things to friends, and donate items to Goodwill and other charities, who can sell them and put the money to good use. Downsize, eliminate, simplify. I promise, you will sleep better at night.

I had a recurring nightmare that was a wake-up call for me. In the dream, I was standing on a corner in New York City, and I had all my possessions in my arms. Things were falling out of my arms, and I was trying to gather them up and cross the street. I'd pick one thing up and another thing would fall to the ground. I couldn't move across the street because I couldn't get all my possessions gathered in my arms at one time. I recognized that I was burdened deep down with "stuff" and that it was preventing me from moving ahead.

I suggest you get involved in a cause that you

are passionate about because of your tragedy. Victor Frankl advised: "Bear witness to the uniquely human potential at its best, which is to transform a personal tragedy into a triumph, to turn one's predicament into a human achievement."

Organizations such as MADD (Mothers Against Drunk Drivers) were started by one person who took tragedy and made something positive come from it. There are many organizations that achieve great things in the world that were born out of tragedy. I became very interested in promoting the use of DNA sampling in our legal system. England has been "DNA fingerprinting" everyone arrested for a felony since 1997 and has experienced a significant increase in the solution rates of crimes. They use DNA as a *crime-solving* tool.

The United States is very far behind in using this technology and primarily uses DNA as a *prosecutorial* tool. Today, fewer than thirty states require some form of "DNA fingerprinting" upon arrest for a felony. Anyone arrested for a federal crime is automatically DNA fingerprinted, but states have been slow to implement this procedure. We have a national DNA database, but there is not much data in it yet since each state can choose to participate or not in the database. Progress is slowly being made to enact this type of law in all states.

I've had the opportunity to speak before state

legislatures considering a DNA fingerprint law with some success. I became aware of this deficiency because of my tragedy, which gave me the credentials and the knowledge to want to change things. Get involved and give purpose to your suffering.

Someone once said, "Sometimes, you have to be flat on your back before you finally look up." The best component to stopping the fall is to invest time in your spiritual journey. Spend time with God. It is common for us to be like little children. When we feel safe and secure, we wander from our parents and stretch our independence. When danger looms, we retreat back to the safety of our parents. A mother bear with her cubs illustrates the same thing. The cubs wander about, brave and courageous, but the moment they meet with danger, they rush back to the safe haven of the mother bear. Regretfully, I can be much the same way in my relationship to God. When things are going well, I tend to neglect my relationship with Him and think I can handle things just fine on my own.

It's important to maintain our communion with God at all times. Never wander very far from Him. Make it a spiritual discipline to set aside time each day to read the Bible, pray, and talk to God, your Father. I found setting time aside in the morning before I go out the door to deal with the world was the best time for me to have a serious talk with my Father.

With the encouragement of friends, I became very serious about my spiritual journey, so I spent three months in the YWAM Crossroads Discipleship Training Program. My spiritual journey moved ahead by light-years.

I don't know the medical theory behind this, but I found that after the shock of tragedy, my short-term memory was pretty useless. A good friend reached out and invited me to have lunch. I completely forgot and remembered only when he called me to see why I hadn't shown up. This happened three times in a row, on three different days with this same friend. He quit asking me, and I think he was offended that I missed three lunch appointments in a row. My memory had always been like a steel trap, but after we lost JonBenét, I couldn't remember things. Make it a point to write things down, tape notes to the door, or your forehead—whatever it takes to aid your damaged short-term memory. It will return to normal, but not for a while.

Often when we are feeling depressed, we think buying something new will make us happy. Yes, it does distract us, but only for a short time. I heard someone say once, "To be happy for a week, buy a new suit. To be happy for a month, buy a new car.

To be happy for a year, get married." This person obviously had a dim view of marriage. The point is, you can't buy happiness. Things and acquisitions distract you for only a moment. It's best to put your checkbook away.

Finally, don't resist the help and companionship of friends who reach out to you. You will find that some of your friends can't handle your grief. You're not so much fun to be around anymore, and friends will fall away. That's not your fault and don't think less of those friends who do not hang in there with you. Those who stick with you are real, lifelong friends. Go out to dinner when they invite you, even if you don't feel like it. You will be glad you did in the end. It's part of adding new memories to your memory bank. I felt for a long time that I was always on the receiving end of my friends' giving. I didn't have the capacity or the will to give in return. That's okay. Don't be resistant to accepting the giving of others. You will have the opportunity to give back when you have recovered.

The good news is that you will recover. There is a beginning and an end to suffering. And you *will* reach the other side.

CHAPTER 30

Engaging in Life Again

*Be anxious for nothing, but in everything
by prayer and supplication, with thanksgiving,
let your requests be made known to God; and the peace
of God, which surpasses all understanding, will
guard your hearts and minds through Christ
Jesus.*

—Philippians 4:6–7

In 2004, when Patsy was still alive, friends suggested that I ought to consider running for political office. I laughed. Me? The one who disliked the political personality to start with and who had disdain for big government become a politician? Nothing could have been farther from my mind. My friends said, "Well, you have great name recognition!" Talk about making lemonade out of lemons! Yes, I needed to reengage in life, but this would be like jumping into a pool of alligators while learning to swim again. The position I was encouraged to seek was state representative for the 105th district of Michigan. The district comprised five counties in Northern Michigan, one of which was Charlevoix County, where we were living. Eighty-five thousand people lived in this mostly rural area made up of small communities, conservative farmers, and small businesses.

Patsy and I met with the chairman of the Republican Party in Charlevoix County, John Haggard. John listened to me without judgment and told me, "If you run for political office in Northern Michigan, you will have to go door-to-door and be in lots of parades." I think John understood that I would be reluctant to throw myself into the public arena after the years of assault we had endured in the media. I was more than reluctant. I told John, "If I go door-to-door and ride or march in parades, I'm liable to get pelted with tomatoes!"

Nevertheless, I joined the race. There were five other candidates who were seeking the party nomination. I had three months to campaign before the primary election. I had no idea what I was getting myself into but I had a strong encourager behind me: I believed in the saying "Behind every successful man is an amazing woman." Patsy immediately began ordering T-shirts, buttons, balloons, and yard signs. Her enthusiasm was contagious.

I drove to the state capital in Lansing to meet with the party machine. They met my candidacy with open skepticism. *Didn't I understand what the world thought of me? No one wins an election in Northern Michigan unless they are a local, someone who is born here.* That cool reception just ignited the independent, I-can-show-you streak in me. I was in the race and I was going to win. As I began to dig into the issues, I became convinced that a businessman in the state legislature could be effective. Michigan had lots of big problems that were going to require major changes to fix. I got excited about trying to make a difference. It would be like trying to save a failing business. I'd done that before and I figured the fundamentals were much the same. Get expenses in line with income.

I prepared to do my first parade, along with Patsy, my campaign manager, and a half-dozen volunteers. I would be putting myself out there, without reservation, and would be forced to deal directly with whatever the world wanted to throw at me. Patsy was in the midst of chemotherapy treatments for the recurrence of her cancer, but here she was, supporting me with all her heart. She never once complained.

Parades are big in Northern Michigan in the summer. Every town festival has a parade. Fire trucks, police cars, high school bands, Boy Scouts, kids on decorated bicycles, and of course, politicians. We had my Ford F-150 truck towing a decorated float.

A country and western singer friend had written a musical jingle for my campaign, and it played loudly on the portable boom box we'd strapped to the top of the pickup. (I know it annoyed the other candidates, as they sarcastically sang along with the tune.) The parade began, and Patsy and I walked behind the float with buckets of candy to pass out to the hundreds of kids that lined both sides of the street. "Isn't this a blast?" Patsy laughed, and it was a blast. People were wonderful. They clapped and shouted words of encouragement. The kids squealed with excitement as they gathered in the candy. Not one tomato was thrown. Not one ugly word was hurled. I put myself out there, exposed, and I received nothing but kindness and encouragement.

As the campaign went on, people came to my side to support me. Key people endorsed my candidacy. (I believed that God opens doors and it is our responsibility to go through those doors.) God seemed to be opening this door wide. Maybe being in politics was what God had planned for me. This beautiful verse in Jeremiah was framed on my bedroom chest of drawers and seemed to be very appropriate for what was happening:

For I know the plans I have for you,
 Plans to prosper you and not to harm you
 Plans to give you hope and a future (NIV).
—Jeremiah 29:11

On the day before the primary election, I knocked on my last door at about three in the afternoon. I had knocked on hundreds of doors and spoken to countless individuals, senior citizens groups, and special-interest organizations. I learned you never can do everything that needs to be done in a political race; you just do as much as you can.

Patsy was a door-to-door warrior. I would always bypass a house when there was one of my opponents' yard signs in the front yard. Patsy wouldn't. More than once I saw her go knock on the door of someone who was obviously supporting one of my opponents. Invariably she would be invited inside and come back out in five or ten minutes with the homeowner putting up one of my signs in his yard instead.

We had worked hard and the pollsters were saying the race was too close to call. There was a lot of media interest in the race, and we had a gathering of about a hundred friends and supporters waiting that evening for the election results. A couple of satellite TV trucks were parked outside our temporary campaign headquarters. I spoke to the group of friends late in the evening and told them it was indeed too close to call and we would have to wait until morning to get the results. The group still resounded with encouragement. I wasn't hopeful. The next morning it was final. Out of 19,000 votes cast, I had lost by 500 votes.

Of course I was disappointed, and I talked to the Lord about it. "God, it seemed like you were opening this door for me, and now it's closed. I'm confused." As I thought about it more, I realized God did open this door and intended me to go through it, but the purpose of the door was to help me reengage in life, not to make me a state representative. Putting myself out in the public without fear was a bridge I needed to cross in my recovery process. By going through this door, I learned that I could be in public without fear, and people didn't view me as a bad person. That was the lesson I think God wanted me to learn.

I believe as part of reengaging in life, we can't be passive. I'm reminded of the joke about a guy who is adrift in a rowboat about to go over the Niagara Falls. A man on the bank offers to throw him a rope. The stranded man says, "No, thank you, I trust in God. I'll be okay." A moment later a helicopter hovers over the rowboat and offers to lower a rope ladder. "No, thank you, I trust in God." Eventually the man goes over the falls to his death, and when he comes before the Lord, he asks, "Why didn't you save me? I trusted in you and I went over the falls anyway." God replied, "Good Heavens, man, I sent a fellow with a rope, I sent a helicopter. You've got to do your part."

CHAPTER 31

Becoming a Whole Person

We all, with unveiled face, beholding as in a mirror the glory of the Lord, are being transformed into the same image from glory to glory...
—2 Corinthians 3:18

I'm having dinner in a restaurant in Charlevoix with good friends who live year-round here in this small Lake Michigan resort town. Two couples and me. We're sitting around a big round table at the Weathervane Restaurant overlooking the river. I'm having French onion soup. We've been talking about travel, about boats, about health ("Did you hear about so-and-so's stroke?"), and the autumn weather. Two husbands, two wives, and one widower. *Widower* is an odd word, sounds like some tool you'd get at Home Depot. I half listened to my friends' conversation, every once in a while giving out a laugh to join theirs.

"Oh, that's a riot. Isn't that a riot, John?"

"Sure is," and I'd shake my head as if I knew what they were laughing about.

"That's life, isn't it just?"

I look up at that comment. I pull a string of mozzarella from my spoon. That's life?

I had owned three homes in this little lakeside town, our first one being a large white Victorian house I thought we'd keep in the family forever, and one day our children and then our children's children would inherit it. It was the home we remodeled with the big front porch Patsy always wanted. I planted red roses on the steep part of the embankment, and it was the perfect setting for Fourth of July parties and family gatherings.

We had been coming up here for almost ten years in the summers—happy, happy times. I sold that house when the media invaded Charlevoix, as it offered no protection from their prying cameras.

Johnny Bee is on the back of my bike, Patsy and Burke close behind us. We're pedaling on the bicycle path. My daughter is singing and chattering behind me as we sail along the path. The sky is bright and the air crisp. We ride to the end of the rock jetty where the lighthouse stands, its red dome rooftop dull from the battering of the Lake Michigan winter storms. My five-year-old, in her yellow cotton sunsuit with the bluebell print, throws her arms around me so I can lift her up to the ground. Her strong little legs wrap around my neck as she sits on my shoulder. She hangs on to my hair for balance.

"Can we play on the spinning top, Dad?"

"Sure," and JonBenét and Burke run together across the sand to the children's playground and start pushing the merry-go-round the kids get spinning and then hop on, hoping not to fall off.

"Push us, Dad!"

And I give the spinning top a push, stand back, and watch my little girl, pigtails flying, and my little boy, his face turned up and laughing, holding on to the bars, going around and around on the disk. This moment now, in the sand at the water's edge, my children begging to go around once more. Pure happiness.

The five of us finish our meal at the Weathervane, hugs, handshakes, good friends, good food, good conversation; the sun has set and the river moves black as patent leather beneath the nearby drawbridge. We walk to the parking lot. More good-byes, "Take care," "be sure to call," "so good to see you," another hug, another handshake. I was about to be alone again as I have been on many similar nights. There was a hole in my life I wanted to fill. Psalm 88:18 laments, "Loved one and friend You have put far from me, *And* my acquaintances into darkness."

I've observed that frequently men who are widowers remarry quickly. I think they feel they're half persons desperately seeking to be whole again. I've learned it's important to become a whole person first, and then and only then, be open to the idea of sharing life with someone.

I stand in the parking lot of the restaurant with my hand on the door handle of my car. I stare at my hand. I don't open the door. I feel like walking. Walking to the bike path, to the merry-go-round, to the white arbor leading up the slope to the big white Victorian lake house. God, I feel like walking home.

CHAPTER 32

Touches from God

*The LORD is near to those
who have a broken heart.*
—Psalm 34:18

On a gray day in November last year I visited the Saint James Cemetery, where Beth, JonBenét, and Patsy are buried. It was chilly and cloudy when I drove through the old cemetery gates, which have been guarding this cemetery for 150 years. I parked the car and walked along the wet gravel to the three gravestones; Beth, JonBenét, Patsy. The old dogwood tree beside the grave sparkled with hanging decorative ornaments left by well-wishers. A lot of people have visited JonBenét's grave.

These small angels, stars, and trinkets they hang on the tree remind me that my fellow man cares and is capable of great compassion. Oddly enough, I always receive an uplifting feeling just to see my loved ones' names engraved on the granite headstones. I kneel beside each marker, rest my hand on it, stay awhile, talk. But to whom? My loved ones aren't here, and their absence is as cold as the earth. I brush leaves and dust from the headstones and remember. I remember the uniformed police standing at parade rest as Patsy's hearse passed on its route from the church to the cemetery. I remember the hands reaching out to touch the casket, to say good-bye, the mounds of flowers, overwhelmingly fragrant in the summer heat. That little tiara of JonBenét's, the reflection of light on the brass handles of the casket that held Beth.

The wind began to rustle the dried leaves still clinging to the old dogwood, and the sun broke through the swiftly moving clouds. I stood in the welcome warmth of the sun, unmoving, and then the sky began to clear, almost as though God had simply brushed the clouds aside. This cemetery could have been the most forlorn place in the world, I thought, yet it wasn't. Each headstone represented a life, someone who was loved, someone who had a past and a family.

I stood by Patsy's headstone with a heavy heart,

when a lone sparrow emerged from the nearby woods and flew right up to me. It flapped its wings and hovered just inches from my chest for what seemed like minutes. I didn't do anything to brush it away; I just stood there. Was it trying to tell me something there in the silence of the cemetery? I thought, wouldn't that be just like the Lord to send a little sparrow to assure me He's taking good care of my girls?

The sparrow flew off, and I knew something significant had just happened. The experience reminded me again of God's smallest blessings. A little sparrow took a moment to be with me at my loved ones' graves to remind me that there is a God in whom I can trust, and who has my loved ones in his care.

CHAPTER 33

Can I Be Happy Again?

*Oh, magnify the LORD with me,
And let us exalt His name together.
I sought the LORD, and He heard me,
And delivered me from all my fears.*
—Psalm 34:3–4

Was there a time during this walk through the valley that I wanted life to be over? I would be less than honest if I said anything other than yes. When the pain from the loss was so intense, I would pray, "Lord, just get me out of here. Take me home. I'm tired of life." Living seemed hopeless and useless. I wanted the pain to end. I saw no end to the suffering. My life as I knew it seemed to be over.

There were those times when suicide seemed

plausible. If God wouldn't take me home, I could take care of it myself, but nothing could be more selfish and cruel to those who loved me: my children, my friends, Patsy. I mentioned one day to Patsy, "Boy, I'm about ready to check out of this place." Patsy rose up, eyebrows raised, "Don't you dare leave me with this mess!" We both laughed, and that was the end of that.

I needed to do as God told Job to do—quit bellyaching and "gird up your loins…Brace yourself like a man." I'm thankful God did not answer my desperate prayer in those dark days to take me home. I am a different person now.

If I were to compose for you a Christmas letter at this time, I'd begin by telling you about my children's lives today, how my daughter, Melinda, married a good man and they have given me three healthy grandsons. I'd tell you that Melinda is an amazing mother and I couldn't be prouder of her. Though I couldn't explain it in a simple Christmas letter, I'd tell you that the relationship between a father and a daughter is very special, and I'd express the joy Melinda brings me when I see her and her family moving ahead in life with order and happiness. My grandsons are happy to see me whenever I'm visiting, and they are eager to show me their latest successes in life.

I would also tell you how my son John Andrew

has matured into a strong, responsible young father, and he and his incredible wife have built a family and loving home. He handled the stress placed on our family very well, and when I visit him and his young family, I experience the same excitement and joy when playing with their children as I did with my own little ones. John Andrew is a profound blessing to his dad.

And then I'd tell you about my youngest son, Burke, who was thrust into the tabloid world as such a young boy. He graduated from Purdue University with a degree in computer information technology, and now holds a very responsible position with a medical records software company. He's an athletic young man with a great sense of humor. We are a tightly knit family and spend our holidays together. Though scattered around the country, we're never far apart. And I'd sign it, Merry Christmas and much love, the Ramseys.

How can I tell you how deeply I love my children, and how they made my life worth living when I felt like dying? How can I tell you how they bless me every day of my new life?

Christmas can be a joyful time again.

CHAPTER 34

A New Beginning

I waited patiently for the LORD;
And He inclined to me,
And heard my cry.
He also brought me up out of a horrible pit,
Out of the miry clay,
And set my feet upon a rock,
And established my steps.
He has put a new song in my mouth—
Praise to our God;
Many will see it and fear,
And will trust in the LORD.

—Psalm 40:1–3

Christmas 2010

Christmas carols float through the rooms of Melinda's home with her husband and three boys. The children sit on the floor with their dad and Burke playing Monopoly in their cozy living room. I sit on the sofa with Melinda, enjoying the warmth and ease of my family. We've been skiing and sledding, and we're all pink-cheeked and exhilarated.

Outside the wind blows tufts of snow, forming waves, ridges, and gullies across the property like the underside of a mammoth white sea. Snowplows have cleared the roads and streets, creating high snowbanks, so that as far as the eye can see, the world is buried in white. "The children love days like this," Melinda is saying, "fresh snow to slide and play in." She is dedicated to her children, just as Patsy was to ours.

I hum with the music. *"Hark the herald angels sing..."*

One of the boys gives a shout. He just bought Boardwalk. The others groan.

We're having Christmas dinner—marinated grilled elk steaks. Melinda passes me an appetizer: antelope sausage and crackers. I joke that this is like the Wild West in the old days when everybody hunted and trapped for their food. We've talked to John Andrew and his family in Colorado by televideo conferencing. I was able to see and wish his children a Merry Christmas (me, a proud grandpa of five children!).

I'm a blessed man. Each of my children is doing well, and my grandchildren are healthy, delightful, and happy. My brother, Jeff, called to wish me a

"Merry Christmas" and to say that his family is healthy and happy.

It's been a long journey to this December twenty-fifth, 2010, here in my children's home, where I feel at peace sitting by the Christmas tree and am able to sing along with Christmas carols and laugh and eat elk steak and lemon cake, and share presents with my loved ones. It's the first Christmas since 1996 when I feel like things are happy again. The dread is gone, the tears have dried, and it's again a joyful time.

I've taken the journey back and told you my personal, untold story. As of this writing, I've purchased a modest house I'm remodeling in Charlevoix. (Another chance to "work like a Bulgarian!") I'm finding goodness in every day. I'm feeling much acceptance and love. The heaviness has left me like the shedding of a bulky winter coat. It gives me a good feeling, this heavy coat falling from me. Life feels good now.

I've been able to work as a business consultant, primarily with young CEOs of small companies. My longtime good friend, Mike Bynum, who selflessly did so much for me and our family throughout our ordeal, enticed me to join his company and oversee marketing and investor relations. I've also been invited to help staff a YWAM Crossroads

Discipleship Training Program next year, the same program I went through.

Will I return to India?

If God leads me, yes.

There are still the occasional media stories appearing about JonBenét's murder. It remains a fascination as one of the country's most high-profile unsolved murders. Some of the stories now tend to include how wronged we were by the police. We continue to pray for the capture of the murderer. We will never stop.

Have I met the challenge that my friend presented to me five years earlier? The challenge when he told me I needed to get to a point where I believed the best days of my life are ahead of me?

I'm at an age now when I realize the road ahead isn't as endless as it used to be. For some people, getting older is like discovering the routes you've traveled to get somewhere don't go there after all. I've discovered that the shorter road ahead is far more interesting and enticing than I ever imagined. God's grace has come to me through trial, through suffering. We're all desperate for a sense of belonging to the human race, as well as to something bigger than ourselves. It's the final and conclusive knowing of the love of God that we're desperate for.

I've just told you the story I haven't told before. And yes, I believe the best days of my life are ahead of me. I found them on the other side of suffering, where they were waiting.

I'm thankful and I'm ready.

Appendix

"A Clear Case of Media Mayhem," Howard Rosenberg, *Los Angeles Times*

September 28, 1998

In 1996, JonBenét Ramsey, age 6, was beaten over the head and garroted in her parents' Boulder, Colo., home on Christmas night. In the months that followed, her parents were beaten over the head and garroted by the media.

The still-unsolved slaying of the elfin beauty queen initiated one of the foulest, yellowest chapters in contemporary U.S. journalism. As smelly as the media assassination of former Atlanta bombing suspect Richard Jewell. As jarring at times as the ear-splitting TV oompahs parading beside the O. J. Simpson murder case. As contorted as the swollen, shrill, gossip-and-leak reporting helping skew and inflate the Clinton-Lewinsky sex scandal.

The guilty vote was nearly unanimous, for instance, when several hundred community college journalism students were queried about the Ramseys at a regional meeting in Los Angeles on Saturday.

And no wonder, given how the parents have been dragged to a tree and strung up by media—despite never having been arrested or publicly accused by authorities of anything to do with this crime.

The mistreatment ranges from talk-radio ranting to something as subtle as newscasts showing footage or photos of blond JonBenét only in her pageant attire and full makeup, as if her parents had created a seductive mini-harlot and barred her from a normal childhood.

This has nothing to do with the Ramseys' possible guilt or innocence, only with fairness not being extended to them—and to others—who are proved guilty of nothing. You'd think the media would have learned these basic ground rules for decency by now. Instead...

"What we had here was a public lynching," Britisher Michael Tracey said from Boulder, where he has taught journalism at the University of Colorado for a decade.

Hardly less scandalous has been the unconscionable behavior of some of the press toward JonBenét's parents, John and Patricia Ramsey, who by this time are surely viewed by much of America either as having murdered their daughter—for any number of speculated reasons—or having been somehow complicitous in her death.

New DNA Technology Clears the Family of JonBenét Ramsey, Kirk Johnson

July 10, 2008

DENVER—A persistent thread among conspiracy theorists and true-crime bloggers who for years have pondered the murder of JonBenét Ramsey, the child beauty queen found strangled in her family's home in nearby Boulder more than 11 years ago, is that the police and prosecutors inadequately investigated whether her killer was a member of the family.

On Wednesday, the Boulder County district attorney, Mary T. Lacy, said definitively that the whispers about prosecutorial plots and favoritism were fantasy. A new technique of analysis, Ms. Lacy said in a letter to JonBenét's father, John Ramsey, has found DNA traces, unobtainable by earlier methods, of an unidentified male on the long johns JonBenét wore the night she died.

The DNA is not from a member of the Ramsey family and is almost definitely that of the killer, who would have presumably removed or otherwise handled the long johns, Ms. Lacy said.

The genetic material matches that from a drop of blood found on JonBenét's underwear early in the investigation. The authorities determined then that the blood was not from a member of the Ramsey family but could not say whether it came from the killer, Ms. Lacy said.

The letter to Mr. Ramsey said the new evidence "has vindicated your family," adding, "No innocent person should have to endure such an extensive trial in the court of public opinion." It said specifically that neither Mr.

Ramsey nor his wife, Patsy, who died of cancer in 2006, nor their son, Burke, was "under any suspicion in the commission of this crime."

Two years ago, Ms. Lacy's office announced with great fanfare the arrest of a suspect, John M. Karr, after what Ms. Lacy described at the time as "several months of a focused and complex investigation." But Mr. Karr's DNA did not match, and less than two weeks later Ms. Lacy announced that he had been cleared of suspicion.

The methodology that led to Wednesday's announcement, called "touch DNA" analysis, is essentially a way of looking for traces of genetic material that earlier methods would have overlooked.

Ms. Lacy said a private laboratory, the Bode Technology Group of Lorton, Va., had tested material scraped from the waistband of the long johns and found a match with the earlier samples taken from the crotch of the underwear JonBenét wore on the night of the crime.

Office of the District Attorney, Twentieth Judicial District

District Attorney's Media Release clearing Ramsey family:

Boulder district Attorney Mary T. Lacy issues the following announcement with regard to the investigation of the murder of JonBenét Ramsey.

On Dec. 25-26, 1996, JonBenét Ramsey was murdered in the home where she lived with her mother, father and brother. Despite a long and intensive investigation, the death of JonBenét remains unsolved.

The murder has received unprecedented publicity and has been shrouded in controversy. That publicity has led to many theories over the years in which suspicion has focused on one family member or another. However, there has been at least one persistent stumbling block to the possibility of prosecuting any Ramsey family members for the death of JonBenét—DNA.

As part of its investigation of the JonBenét Ramsey homicide, the Boulder police identified genetic material with apparent evidentiary value. Over time, the police continued to investigate DNA, including taking advantage of advances in the science and methodology. One of the results of their efforts was that they identified genetic material and a DNA profile from drops of JonBenét's blood located in the crotch of the underwear she was wearing at the time her body was discovered. That genetic profile belongs to a male and does not belong to anyone in the Ramsey family.

On March 24, 2008, Bode [The Bode Technology Group, Inc., of Lorton, Virginia] informed us that they had recovered and identified genetic material from both sides of the waist area of the long johns. The unknown male profile previously identified from the inside crotch area of the underwear matched the DNA recovered from the long johns at Bode.

We consulted with a DNA expert from a different laboratory, who recommended additional investigation into the remote possibility that the DNA might have come from sources at the autopsy when this clothing was removed. Additional samples were obtained and then analyzed by the Colorado Bureau of Investigation to assist us in this effort. We received those results on June 27th of this year and are, as a result, confident that this DNA did not come from innocent sources at the autopsy. As mentioned above, extensive DNA testing had previously excluded people connected to the family and to the investigation as possible innocent sources.

The unexplained third-party DNA on the clothing of the victim is very significant and powerful evidence. It is very unlikely that there would be an innocent explanation for DNA found at three different locations on two separate items of clothing worn by the victim at the time of her murder. This is particularly true in this case because the matching DNA profiles were found on genetic material from inside the crotch of the victim's underwear and near the waist on both sides of her long johns, and because concerted efforts that might identify a source, and perhaps an innocent explanation, were unsuccessful.

It is therefore the position of the Boulder District Attorney's Office that this profile belongs to the perpetrator of the homicide.

The Boulder District Attorney's Office does not consider any member of the Ramsey family, including John, Patsy or Burke Ramsey, as suspects in this case. We make this announcement now because we have recently obtained this new scientific evidence that adds significantly to the exculpatory value of the previous scientific evidence. We do so with full appreciation for the other evidence in this case.

Local, national and even international publicity has focused on the murder of JonBenét Ramsey. Many members of the public came to believe that one or more of the Ramseys, including her mother or her father, or even her brother, were responsible for this brutal homicide. Those suspicions were not based on evidence that had been tested in court; rather, they were based on evidence reported by the media.

It is the responsibility of every prosecutor to seek justice. That responsibility included seeking justice for people whose reputations and lives can be damaged irreparably by the lingering specter of suspicion. In a highly publicized case, the detrimental impact of publicity and suspicion on people's lives can be extreme. The suspicions about the Ramseys in this case created an ongoing living hell for the Ramsey family and their friends, which added to their suffering from the unexplained and devastating loss of JonBenét.

For reasons including those discussed above, we believe that justice dictates that the Ramseys be treated only as victims of this very serious crime. We will accord them all the rights guaranteed to the victims of violent crimes under the law in Colorado and all the respect and sympathy due from one human being to another. To the extent that this office has added to the distress suffered by the Ramsey family at any time or to any degree, I offer my deepest apology.